D1716727

# 1 Panoramas Overviews, & Vignettes Snap Shots, Apocalypses Unveilings

an exeGeses classic
by Herb Jahn


Published by exeGeses Bibles
Printed in South Korea
ISBN 0—9631951—9—0

EMAIL exegeses@exegesesbibles.org
PHONE 800 9 BIBLE 9
FAX 714 835 1705
WEB www.exegesesbibles.org

Presented to

______________________

on the occasion of

______________________

this ______________________ day

of the ______________________ month

of the ______________________ year

by ______________________

# 3 Prologue

**IMAGINE!** There you are — enthroned on the cathedra of that vast stage called life.

First come the Panoramas — the Overviews of Scripture — from Creation to the Consumation

Then the Vignettes — the Snap Shots of livings — from Friends & Lovers through the Ten Words.

The curtain opens, you see the Apocalypses — the Unveilings of Scripture from aeons past, to the aeons of the aeons fast approaching.

You look upon the lush valleys; you lift your eyes unto the hills; you gaze beyond the heavens; you behold the glory — the shechinah glory!

Each few pages, as a precious brocade, with golden threads interwoven, transport you to a higher level — beginning with Creation of the Universe, and on to the final Halalu Yah, Amen!

This book is so prepared that you may peruse it for just a moment, and lay it down. Or perhaps become so involved that you'll not lay it down — and when you have finished, you'll reread and rereread it again and again.

And consider the possibility of a fringe benefit — that as you allow the Holy Spirit to touch your life, you too may be transported into a new found intimate holy of holies relationship with the holiest of all.

Not only will page after page bless your heart, and loft you to new spiritual heights, even before you finish, you will discover that you will not only have acquired, but will have experienced a knowledge of Scripture beyond your peers.

~~~

My Heavenly Father,

I bring this precious person into your presence, and ask that you libate a libation of anointment on their head til it flows over their total being.

Amen.
~~~

# Format 4

All Scriptures are from the exeGeses parallel Bible, The Aramaic New Covenant, or directly from Hebraic, Aramaic & Hellenic manuscripts.

The exeGeses parallel Bible consists of two Bibles sided by side. In the left column is the exeGeses ready research Bible.

The exeGeses Ready Research Bible, with its myriad exegeses inserted at the point of occurrence, transforms the Authorized King James Version into a Literal Translation & Transliteration.

Here is an example from Psalm 150:
*Praise ye the LORD* **Halalu Yah:**
*Praise God* **Halal El** in his *sanctuary* **holies:**

The plain text is the Authorized King James:
*The oblique text is the Authorized King James under exegeses:*
**The bold text is the exegesis**.

When crucial, you will also see Strong's Concordance Numbers within the text. They have been inserted to help you in your further research for the truth.

The Old Covenant Numbers are within brackets: [0000].

The New Covenant Numbers are within braces: {0000}.

The exeGeses Companion Bible in the right column is an easy reading version containing all the exegeses of the exeGeses ready research Bible.

The Aramaic New Covenant is Translated & Transliterated directly from manuscripts in the language of our Saviour.

May your heart be exulted as you read the legacy of Yah Veh the Eternal Being, and Yah Shua the Eternal Saviour.

# Contents

## Panoramas

# 6

## Vignettes



## Apocalypses

# 7 Panoramas of

Once upon a time — a long, long time ago — I can still hear it ringing in my ears — well, actually nothing's ringing in my ears — except the ringing in my ears — when I was a little boy in kindergarten — that's how Miss Stevenson always began her stories.

Where oh where shall I begin this book? I want to meander back a bit further — actually a lot further. I've got it! How about this?

'In the beginning' — now there's a concept — can't go much further back than that. Oh I know - some 'intellectual scientist' — now there's an oxymoron — like to precede this by a few billion years — give or take a few — but 'In the beginning' — that's how my all time favorite Book begins: Elohim (that's the Hebrew word for the title of God) created the heavens and the earth.

And there he was — he and his Holy Spirit — he and his Word — his living Word. Here's how the Aramaic manuscripts say it:

In the beginning,<br>
the Word having been,<br>
and the Word having been Elohim,<br>
and Elohim having been the Word,<br>
he , having been in the beginning, unto Elohim,<br>
all through his hand became:<br>
and without him<br>
not even one being whatever became.

It's one of those, 'You had to be there to appreciate it' kind of experience. But you would not have experienced all that much, because darkness covered the the abyss.

Now follow me on this — like a loving mother hen, exactly as the Saviour would have gathered Yeru Shalem —the Spirit of Elohim brooded over the face of the waters.

And Elohim said, "Light, be!" — and light became.

And Elohim said, "Expanse, be midst the waters." — and the expanse became.

And Elohim said, "Waters under the heavens, congregate unto one place, and dry, be seen." — and it became.

And he called the dry, Earth, and he called the congregating of the waters, Seas — and it became.

And Elohim said, "Lights, be in the expanse of the heavens." — and they became.

And Elohim said, "Waters, teem with teemers having a living soul, and flyers to fly above the earth on the face of the expanse of the heavens."

And Elohim created great monsters, and every living soul that creeps in species, and every winged flyer in species.

And Elohim said, "Earth, bring forth the living soul in species, animals and creepers and live beings of the earth in species." And it became.

# Creation 8

And Elohim said, Let us work 'adam' — that's Hebraic for 'human' — in our image, after our likeness: and let them dominate over the fish of the sea, and over the flyers of the heavens, and over the animals, and over all the earth, and over every creeper creeping upon the earth.

And as a little child on the beach gathers the sand to make castles of dreams, Elohim took of the dust of the soil, and formed an adam. And Elohim puffed into this dust of the soil, and this adam became a living soul.

And Elohim planted a garden in Eden — a Paradise beyond human description.

What a life!

And Elohim said, "Not good for adam to be alone" — and he created him a help meet.

And Yah Veh Elohim caused a sleep to fall upon Adam, and he slept: and he took one of his ribs, and closed up the flesh underneath thereof; And the rib, which Yah Veh Elohim had taken from this adam, he built a woman, and entered her unto the adam.

And Adam said, This at this time is bone of my bones, and flesh of my flesh: this shall be called Woman, because was taken out of Man. And Adam called the name of his woman Chavvah; because of being the mother of all living.

Imagine!
Elohim the Creator,
His Word the Saviour,
His Creation and His Creatures.

What a relationship! What a life!

Just imagine, two people — the only people in the whole wide world — in the Paradise of Eden — with one restriction, and they couldn't handle it.

And on the seventh day, Elohim finished his work, and shabbathized*.

*verb of Shabbath

## AND NOW — THE BAD NEWS!

This serpent comes along, gets Chavvah to disobey Elohim, and alters the course of all humanity to the aeons.

## THEN COMETH THE CATACLYSM

And from then on, it was all downhill. Because shortly thereafter, Elohim said, "My Spirit shall not always strive with humanity." And Elohim set out to destroy all humanity from the face of the earth —

BUT a man named Noach found grace in the sight of Elohim.

And if it were not for that, you and I and a lot of other folks would not be here today.

# 9 Panoramas of

And exactly as Elohim instructed, he built this great big box — which we call an ark — and filled the hold of the box with lives of all species. And to his family, he might well have said, "All aboard" — even though the box was sitting on dry ground.

What followed was a rather eventful forty days and forty nights — first a drizzle — then the downpour — then a stillness.

At long last, the box rests on Mount Ararat. And Noach opens the windows and sends forth a raven which flew away, and having no place to land, returned.

Then Noach sends forth a dove — and having no place to land, also returns.

So Noach waits seven days, and again he sends forth a dove, and in the evening, returns with a plucked olive leaf — so Noach knew that the waters had abated from off the earth. And after seven days, he sends forth the dove that never returned.

And there Noach was — he and his — and all the world was wiped out — and here we are!

## PROCLAMATION

Let all humanity know, as evidenced by my existence, as evidenced by my presence in your sight, that I am a descendant of Noach — and have been spared of the dire results of the cataclysm.*

*The new Covenant word for flood.

## THE COVENANT OF THE RAINBOW

And I shall raise my covenant with you; neither shall all flesh be cut off any more by the waters of a flood; neither shall there any more be a flood to ruin the earth.

And Elohim said, This is the sign of the covenant which I give between me and between you and between every living soul that is with you for generations to the aeons:

I do give my bow in the cloud, and it shall be for a sign of a covenant between me and between the earth. And it shall become, when I overcloud an overclouding upon the earth, that the bow shall be seen in the cloud:And I shall remember my covenant, which is between me and between you and between every living soul of all flesh; and the waters shall no more become a flood to ruin all flesh.

And the bow shall be in the cloud; and I shall look upon it, that I may remember the covenant of the aeons between Elohim and between every living soul of all flesh that is upon the earth.

# Creation 10

## AND THE BIG BAD BOMB WENT BOOM!

This second epistle, beloved, Petros even now scribed unto you; to rouse your sincere minds in reminding — that you may remember the rhema which were foretold through the holy prophets, and of the mizvah of us the apostles of our Adonay and Saviour: Knowing this firstly, that there shall come upon the final days mockers, journeying through their own personal private pantings, and wording, Where is the pre—evangelism of his parousia? Indeed from when the fathers were put to sleep, all thus abide as from the beginning of the creation.

Indeed they have willed to hide this, that by the word of Elohim the heavens were of old, and the earth standing from the water and through the water: Through which the world then, being flooded with water, destructed:

But the heavens, and the earth, now, by the same word are treasured, guarded unto fire unto the day of justice and destruction of irreverent humanity.

## I PREDICT

Of the day and the hour of Yah Shua's parousia, or of the Day of Yah, no one knows — except the Father. But here is a clue — are you able to detect it?

But, beloved, may none of you hide this one, that one day by Yah Veh is as a thousand years, and a thousand years as one day. Yah Veh delayeth not his pre—evangelism (as some deem delay); but is patient unto us, having willed that none destruct, but that all come pass into repentance.

Think me not audacious when I say I know exactly when these events are about to occur — its when the final person to be saved, has been saved — and that is the hour we know not.

# 11 Panoramas of

## THE BIG BANG IS NOT A THEORY

Its just that the psuedo scientist put it in the beginning of creation, instead of at the end.

Is it not strange, how humanity if his wisdom gets it all backwards? While they effort to comprehend and/or surpass the mind of Elohim, they have arrived at the conclusion became through a big bang — not considering for a moment that is how the creation will cease to exist.

## THE DAY OF YAH VEH

But the day of Yah Veh shall come as a thief in the night; in the which the heavens shall pass with a whir, then the elements, being causticized shall disintegrate, and also the earth and the works that are therein it shall be burned up.

So concerning all these being disintegrated, what ever must ye be in holy behavior and reverence, awaiting and hasting unto the parousia of the day of Elohim, through which the heavens being fiery shall be disintegrated, and the elements being causticized shall melt down?

## THE NEW HEAVENS AND THE NEW EARTH

And I saw the new heavens and the new earth: Indeed the first heavens and the first earth were passed; and there became no more sea.

## THE NEW YERU SHALEM

And I Yah Chanan saw the holy city, new Yeru Shalem, coming descending from Elohim from the heavens, prepared as a bride adorned for her man.

And he bore me in spirit upon a mega and high mountain, and shewed me that mega city, the holy Yeru Shalem, descending from the heavens from Elohim, Having the glory of Elohim: and her light like unto a stone most precious, even like a jasper stone, crystaline;

Also having a wall mega and high, having twelve gates, and over the gates twelve angels, and names epigraphed, which of the twelve tribes of the sons of Yisra El: By the east three gates; by the north three gates; by the south three gates; and by the west three gates.

And the wall of the city had twelve foundations, and in them the names of the twelve apostles of the Lamb.

# Creation 12

## THE MEASUREMENTS OF THE NEW YERU SHALEM

And he that spake with me had a golden reed so as to measure the city, and the gates thereof, and the wall thereof.

And the city setteth foursquare, and the length of it is as long as broad: and he measured the city with the reed, over twelve thousand stadia. The length and the breadth and the height of it being equal. And he measured the wall thereof, an hundred forty four cubits, — the measure of a human, that is, of the angel.

## THE MATERIALS OF THE NEW YERU SHALEM

And the structure of the wall of it having been jasper: and the city pure gold, like unto pure glass. And the foundations of the wall of the city adorned with all precious stones. The first foundation jasper; the second, sapphire; the third, a chalcedony; the fourth, an emerald; the fifth, sardonyx; the sixth, sardius; the seventh, chrysolite; the eighth, beryl; the ninth, a topaz; the tenth, a chrysoprasus; the eleventh, a jacinth; the twelfth, an amethyst.

And the twelve gates, twelve pearls; each and every one gate having been of one pearl: and the broadway of the city pure gold, as it were diaphanous glass.

## YOUR FIRST MEMORY LESSON

I am Elohim's creation
I'll live it:
I am Elohim' likeness
I'll look it:
I am Elohim's image
I'll bear it:
I am Elohim's glory
I'll reflect it.

# 13 Panoramas of

## TITLES OF THE CREATOR: GOD

Several Hebraic and Aramaic words are all translated by the single English word, God. Here they are as presented in the Concordance:
[410] **El** from [352]. Also translated as mighty, almighty.

**OLD COVENANT:**
- [426] **Elahh** Aramaic
- [430] **Elohim** plural of [433].
- [433] **Elohh**

**NEW COVENANT:**
- {1682} **Eloi** from the Aramaic [426]
- {2316} **Theos**

**Deity** presented himself with the plural **Elohim** in the very first sentence of Scripture. He further emphasised this when he said, "Let **us** make humanity in **our** image and **our** likeness." We also learn, in this first sentence that the Spirit is a part of this plurality. And as we explore Scripture, we learn that the Word in bodily form completes the plurality of **Elohim** — which some refer to as the triune Deity.

## TITLES OF DEITY: LORD

**OLD COVENANT: HEBRAIC and ARAMAIC:**
- [113] **Adon, Adoni** is a title refering to anyone of high rank, whether landlord, a woman's man (wife's husband) (neither **wife** nor **husband** appear in Scripture), or English politics. Sarah called Abraham her lord,
- [136] **Adonay** an emphatic form of [113], refers only to Deity.

In verses with the words, **Lord God**, Lord is [136], and God is a mistranslation of [3068].

At one time, [113] and [136] word the same word — but humanity, in its frailty, efforted to distinguish between Deity and humanity. And in their frailty, erred.

In Psalm 110:1, for example, as most Versions mistranslate, The LORD [3068] said unto my Lord [113], [113] definitely refers to Adonay the Saviour.

This verse is of such import that it is repeated four times in the New Covenant.

# Titles 14

**TITLES OF DEITY: LORD**
**NEW COVENANT: HELLENIC**
also known as Bible Greek:

•{2962} **kurios** *noun* God, Lord, LORD, master, sir.

Whereas the Old Covenant translators, in their frailty, attempted to distinguish between Deity [136] and humanity [113], the New Covenant translators used one word {2962} to refer the **title** of Deity [430], the **name** of Deity [3068], the title of the Saviour, and folks in authority.

Even our Aramaic manuscripts failed to distinguish.

In the four mistranslations of Psalm 110:1, the Authorized King James Version did supply a clue: They did translate [1962] as LORD (large and small caps) which would refer to the **Name** of Deity.

So how is a person able to distinguish between all the above? Only by a thorough knowledge of both the Old Covenant and the New Covenant.

# 15 Panoramas of

## I AM THAT I AM

**AM, ARE and IS**

As you examine the word **am** in your concordance, you will see very few numbers. This means that the verbs were not in the original manuscripts, but supplied by the translators. The Hebrew tongue would never squander the verb **am** by saying, I **am** going to the city — but rather, I go to the city.

The word **am**, in the Hebrew is very powerful — declaring the status of **existence** and of **being**.

•[1961] **Hayah** to exist, to be.
**Hayah** is also the root of the personal name of Elohim.

In the New Covenant, **I AM** is expressed with two words:
•{1472{ **ego** personal pronoun, I
•{1510} **eimi** AM to exist, to be

## THE CREATOR REVEALS HIMSELF AS I AM WHO I AM

**Exodus 3:11—15**

And Mosheh said unto Elohim, Behold, when I enter unto the sons of Yisra El, and shall say unto them, The Elohim of your fathers hath sent me unto you; and they shall say to me, What is his name? what shall I say unto them?

And Elohim said unto Mosheh, **I AM** WHO **I AM**: and he said, Thus shalt thou say unto the sons of Yisra El, **I AM** hath sent me unto you.

And Elohim said again unto Mosheh, Thus shalt thou say unto the sons of Yisra El, The Yah Veh Elohim of your fathers, the Elohim of Abraham, the Elohim of Yizchaq, and the Elohim of Ya'aqov, hath sent me unto you: this is my name to the aeons, and this is my memorial unto all generations.

# Titles 16

## THE SAVIOUR REVEALS HIMSELF AS I AM

**Yah Chanan** 4:26 **I AM** hath spoken unto thee.
6:20 **I AM**; be not awestricken.
6:35, 41, 48, 51 **I AM** the bread of life:
8:12 **I AM** the light of the world
8:18 **I AM** witnesseth concerning myself, and the Father that sent me witnesseth concerning me. 24 unless ye trust that **I AM**, ye shall die in your sins.
8:28 When ever ye have lifted the Son of humanity, then shall ye know that **I AM** .
8:58 Ere Abraham became, **I AM**.
10:7 because **I AM** the portal of the sheep.
10:11, 14 **I AM** the good tender:
11:25 **I AM** the resurrection, and the life:
13:19 From now I word you ere it become, so that, whenever it becometh, ye may trust that **I AM**.
14:6 Yah Shua wordeth unto him, **I AM** the way, the truth, and the life:
15:1 **I AM** the true vine, and my Father is the cultivator. 15:5 **I AM** the vine, ye the branches:
18:5 Yah Shua wordeth unto them, **I AM** .
18:6 As soon then as he had said unto them, that **I AM** , they went backward, and fell to the ground.
18:7 Then asked he them again, Whom seek ye? Then they said, Yah Shua the Naziyr. 8 Yah Shua answered, I have said to you that **I AM**:
18:37 Thou wordest because **I AM** a sovereign.
**Matthaios** 14:27 But straightway Yah Shua spake unto them, wording, Courage! **I AM**! Awe not.
22:32 **I AM** Elohim of Abraham and the Elohim of Yizchaq, and the Elohim of Ya'aqov? Elohim is not the Elohim of the dead, but of the living.
**Apocalypse** 1:8 **I AM** Alpha and Omega, the beginning and the shalom, wordeth Adonay, the being, and the having been, and the coming being; Shadday. 1:11 **I AM** Alpha and Omega, the first and the final: 1:17 **I AM** the first and the final:
2:23 And I shall slaughter her children in death; and all the congregations/ecclesiae shall know that **I AM** — which searcheth the reins and hearts: and I shall give unto each of you according to your works.
22:6 And he said unto me, It hath become. **I AM** Alpha and Omega, the beginning and the shalom. I shall give unto him that is athirst of the fountain of the water of life gratuitously.
22:13 **I AM** Alpha and Omega, the beginning and the shalom, the first and the final.
**I AM** the root and the genus of David, the radiant and dawning star.

# 17 Panoramas of

## TITLE OF THE SAVIOUR IS HA MASHIYACH

**OLD COVENANT:**
•[4886] **mashach** *verb* to anoint
•[4899] **Mashiyach** *noun* anointed one, ha Mashiyach

**NEW COVENANT**
•{5548} **chrio** *verb* anoint
•{5547} **Christos** *noun* a Hellenic translation from the Hebraic Mashiyach[4899]: anointed one,ha Mashiyach
•{3323} **Messias** *noun* a transliteration from the Hebraic Mashiyach [4899].
NOTE: Christ is a translation from the Hellenic Christos, which is a translation from the Hebraic Mashiyach.

**Psalm 2:2** The sovereigns of the earth station themselves, and the potentates counsel unitedly, against Yah Veh, and against his anointed [4899]

**Acts 4:26** The sovereigns of the earth presented themselves, and the archons were gathered over him — against Yah Veh, and against his Christ {5547} [4899] Mashiyach.

## A MESSIANIC PROPHECY

**Yesha Yah 61:1, 2** The Spirit of Adonay Yah Veh is upon me; because Yah Veh hath anointed [4886] me to tidings evangelize unto the meek; he hath sent me to bind the crushed in heart, to recall liberty to the captives, and the release of releasing to them that are bound; To recall the year of pleasure of Yah Veh, and the day of vengeance avengement of our Elohim; to sigh over all that mourn;

**Loukas 4:18, 19** The Spirit of Yah Veh is upon me, because he hath anointed {5548} me to evangelize to the poor; he hath apostolized me to cure the shattered heart, to herald forgiveness to the captives, and sight to the blind, to apostolize in forgiveness them that are crushed, To herald the acceptable year of Adonay.

# Titles 18

## THE VISION OF THE SEVENTY SEVENS

**Dani El 9:24—27** Seventy sevens are determined upon thy people and upon thy holy city, to restrain rebellion, and to finish off and seal the sins, and to kaphar/atone for perversity, and to enter justness to the aeons, and to seal the vision and prophecy, and to anoint [4886] the holy of holies.

Know and comprehend, that from the rising of the words to return and to build Yeru Shalem unto ha Mashiyach [4899] the Eminent shall be seven sevens, and sixty and two sevens: the broadway shall be built and restored, and the trench, even in distressful times.

And after sixty and two sevens shall Mashiyach be cut*, but not for himself: and the people of the Eminent that shall enter shall ruin the city and the holies; and the end thereof shall be with a flood, and unto the end of the war devastations are appointed.

*as in cutting a covenant

And he shall empower the covenant with many for one seven: and in the half of the seven he shall shabbathize the sacrifice and the offering, and for the wing of abominations he shall devastate it, even until the final finish, and that appointed shall be flowed upon the devastated.

**Yah Chanan 1:41** He first findeth his own brother Shimon, and wordeth unto him, We have found the Messias {3323} ha Mashiyach [4899], which is , being translated, the Christ {5547} ha Mashiyach [4899].

**Yah Chanan 4:25, 26** The woman wordeth unto him, I know that Messias {3323} ha Mashiyach [4899], cometh, which is worded Christ {5547} ha Mashiyach [4899]: when ever he is come, he shall evangelize us all.

Yah Shua wordeth unto her, {1473} {1510} **I AM** hath spoken unto thee.

# 19 Panoramas of

**Panorama of the Name of the Creator**

Multitudes
by the Myriad
worship a Creator
whose holy Name
has been veiled
from them

**Most Bible Versions Name Diety,
With Large and Small Caps — LORD**

I am the LORD; that is my name.

Problem is, LORD is not a name, but a title.

**OLD COVENANT:**
•[3050} **Yah** is the contracted form of [3068]: Eternal.
**Yah** is also the form used when halaling him — as in **Hallalu Yah**.
•[3068] **Yah Veh** *noun* Eternal being. **Yehovah** is the spelling in Strong's Concordance.
•[1984] **halal** *verb* the highest form of praise; negatively, to boast.

**NOTE:** Strong spells [3050] with an **a**, and [3068] with an **e**, even though it is from the same root. exeGeses Bibles transliterates [3068] as Yah Veh.

# Names 20

**NOTE:** The original Hebraic and Aramaic manuscripts had no vowels. Vowel 'points' were added within the original letters in the Masoretic Text in the eighth century. The vowels were selected by tradition, and chosen at random.

**NOTE:** The Saxons also had a minor influence on the Old Covenant, and a major influence on the New Covenant by changing two letters to conform to their alphabet.

The **V** was changed to **W**, and pronounced as **V**:

The **Y** was changed to **J**, and pronounced as **Y**.

**Psalm 68:4**

Sing to Elohim! Psalm to his name!
Extol him who rides upon the plains,
by his name, Yah,
and jump for joy at his face.

•[3050] **Yah**, •[1984] **Halal**

**Psalm 150:**

Halalu Yah.
Halal El in his holies:
halal him in the expanse of his strength.
Halal him for his might:
halal him according to his myriadfold greatness.
Halal him with the sound of the shophar:
halal him with the bagpipe and harp.
Halal him with the tambourine
and round dance:
halal him with strummers and woodwinds.
Halal him upon the hearkening cymbals:
halal him upon the clanging cymbals.
Let all that breathe halal Yah.
Halalu Yah.

# 21 Panoramas of

**PANORAMA**
**OF THE NAME OF THE CREATOR**

How would you

like to know

your Creator

on a first name basis?

There's an old rumor out there that the name of Yah Veh is too holy to pronounce.

In Deuteronomy 6:13 and 10:20, Yah Veh mizvahs (commands) us to oath by his name:
Thou shalt awe Yah Veh thy Elohim and serve him, and shalt oath by his name.

In Old Covenant times, every covenant had two requirements to validate:

1. cutting the flesh and placing blood on the covenant scribing;
2. oathing in the name of Yah Veh.

Any person who violated the covenant was taken outside the city and stoned. So rather than risking their lives, the Yah Hudiy discontinued the mizvah.

The only restriction, Leviticus 19:12:
And ye shall not oath by my name falsely.

Would you not call your best friend by name — or an endearing nick name?
Would you not call your Creator by his name — if he mizvahed you to?

# Names 22

**Yesha Yah 42:8**

**Most Versions:**
I am the LORD, that is my name.

**exeGeses parallel Bible, left column:**
I *am the LORD* **Yah Veh**, that is my name.

**exeGeses parallel Bible, right column:**
I — Yah Veh, that is my name.

## COMPOUND NAMES OF YAH VEH

**Yah** *tr name* yah [3050] *name* of Deity in basic form: Eternal Existent One.
**Yah Veh** *tr name* yehovah [3068], [3069] Eternal Existent Being.
**Yah Veh Nissi** *tr name* yehovah nissi [3071] Yah Veh Ensign.
**Yah Veh Ra'ah** *tr name* yehovah [3068] raah [7462] Yah Veh Tender; **see** Psalm 23:1.
**Yah Veh Raphah** *tr name* yehovah [3068] raphah [7495] Yah Veh Healer.
**Yah Veh Shalom** *tr name* yehovah shalom [3073] Yah Veh Shalom.
**Yah Veh Sham** *tr name* yehovah [3068] sham [8033] Yah Veh's Presence; **see** Yechezq El 48:35.
**Yah Shua** *tr name* yehowshua [3091] yeshuwa [3442], [3443] ieesous {2424} Yah Saves; the *name* of Mosheh's successor, the *name* of our Adonay Mashiyach, and the *name* of other persons.
**Yah Veh Yireh** *tr name* yehovah yireh [3070] Yah Veh Sees.
**Yah Veh Zabaoth** *tr name* yehovah [3068] zaba'ah [6635] *plural* zaba'oth {4519} Zabaoth Yah Veh of Hosts.
**Yah Veh Zadakah** *tr name* yehovah [3068] Zadakah [6666] Yah Veh of Justness.
**Yah Veh Zidqenu** *tr name* yehovah zidqenuw [3072] a combined form of yehovah [3068] and zedek [6664] Yah Veh of Justness.

# 23 Panoramas of

## PANORAMA
## of the NAME of the CREATOR
## in the NEW COVENANT:

•{2962} **kurios** *noun* God, Lord, LORD, master, sir.

Whereas the Old Covenant translators, in their frailty, attempted to distinguish between Deity [136] and humanity [113], the New Covenant translators used one word {2962} to refer to the **title** of Deity [430], the **name** of Deity [3068], the title of the Saviour, and folks in authority.

Even our Aramaic manuscripts fail to distinguish.

So how is one able to distinguish when {2962} refers to **Yah Veh**?

1. Here's one I discovered, that amazed even my Greek Professor:

In the Novum Testamentum Graece manuscripts, whenever the Saviour is indicated, {2962} is preceded by the article, **the** {3588}: and when the Creator is indicated, the article is omitted — except in the Evangelism of Loukas.

2. By the context — when the New Covenant verse alludes to or quotes and Old Covenant verse.

**Matthaios 4:1—10** Then Yah Shua embarked under the Spirit into the desert to be tested under Satan/Diabolos. And when he had fasted forty days and forty nights, he was afterward famished.

Then Satan/Diabolos taketh him into the Holy city, and setteth him upon a wing of the holies, And wordeth unto him, If thou be the Son of Elohim, cast thyself below: indeed it is scribed, that He shall mizvah his angels concerning thee: and they shall take thee, lest ever thou dash thy foot unto a stone.

Yah Shua said unto him, It is scribed again, Thou shalt not test [3068] {2962} Yah Veh thy Elohim.

Again, Satan/Diabolos taketh him into an exceeding high mountain, and sheweth him all the sovereigndoms of the world, and the glory of them;

And wordeth unto him, All these shall I give thee, If ever thou shalt fall down and worship me.

Then wordeth Yah Shua unto him, Go, Satan: indeed it is scribed, Thou shalt worship Yah Veh [3068] {2962} thy Elohim, and him only shalt thou liturgize.

**Yah Chanan 1:23** He said, I — the voice of one crying in the desert, Straighten the way of *the Lord* Yah Veh [3068] {2962}, exactly as said the prophet Yesha Yah.

### THE TRIUMPHAL ENTRY OF YAH SHUA

**Yah Chanan 12:12, 13** On the morrow vast throngs that were come into the feast , when they heard that Yah Shua was coming into Yeru Shalem, Took branches of phoinix, and departed to meet him, and cried, Hoshia Na! Eulogized the Sovereign of Yisra El that cometh in the name of Yah Veh [3068] {2962}.

**Yah Chanan 12:37** But though he had done so many signs in front of them, yet they trusted not in him: 38 So that the word of Yesha Yah the prophet might be fulfilled, which he said, Yah Veh [3068] {2962}, who hath trusted our report? and to whom hath the arm of Yah Veh [3068] {2962} been unveiled?

**Matthaios 1:24, 25** Then Yoseph being raised from slumber did as the angel of Yah Veh [3068] {2962} had mizvahed him, and took unto him his woman: And knew her not till she had birthed her firstbirthed Son: and he called his name Yah Shua.

### YOSEPH, MIRYAM, AND YAH SHUA FLEE TO MISRAYIM

**Matthaios 2:13, 15** Then when they were departed, Behold! the angel of Yah Veh [3068] {2962} appeareth to Yoseph in a dream, wording, Arise, and take the childling and his mother, and flee into Mizrayim, and be thou there until ever I say to thee: for indeed Herod is about to seek the childling to destroy him. 15 And having been there until the death of Herod: so that it might be fulfilled which was rhetorized of Yah Veh [3068] {2962} through the prophet, wording, From Mizrayim have I called my Son.

### YOSEPH, MIRYAM, AND YAH SHUA GO TO NAZARETH

**Matthaios 2:19** But when Herod had died, Behold! an angel of Yah Veh [3068] {2962} appeareth in a dream to Yoseph in Mizrayim,

**Matthaios 3:3** Indeed this be he that was rhetorized by the prophet Yesha Yah, wording, The voice of one crying in the desert, Prepare ye the way of Yah Veh [3068] {2962}, make his paths straight.

**Romans 11:3** Yah Veh [3068] {2962}, they have slaughtered thy prophets, and digged thine altars; and I am left alone, and they seek my soul.

# 25 Panoramas of

**Hebrews 7:21** (Indeed those priests became apart from an oath; but this with an oath through him that worded unto him, *The Lord* Yah Veh [3068] {2962} oathed and shall not regret, Thou art a priest unto the eons through the order of Malkiy Zedeq:)

**Hebrews 8:2** A liturgist of the holies, and of the true tabernacle, which Yah Veh [3068] {2962} staked, and not humanity.

**Hebrews 8:8—11** Indeed blaming them, he wordeth, Behold! the days come, wordeth Yah Veh [3068] {2962}, when I shall shalam a new covenant upon the house of Yisra El and upon the house of Yah Hudah: Not according to the covenant that I made with their fathers in the day when I seized them by the palm to lead them from the land of Mizrayim; because they abode not in my covenant, and I disregarded them, wordeth Yah Veh [3068] {2962}. Because this is the covenant that I shall cut with the house of Yisra El after those days, wordeth Yah Veh [3068] {2962}; I shall give my torah into their mind, and epigraph them upon their hearts: and I shall be unto them Elohim, and they shall be unto me, people: And they shall never ever doctrinate each his neighbour, and each his brother, wording, Know Yah Veh [3068] {2962}: because all shall know me, from the least until the mega of them.

**Apocalypse 4:11** Thou art worthy O Yah Veh [3068] {2962}, to receive glory and honour and dynamis: because thou hast created all, and through thy pleasure they be and were created.

**Apocalypse 11:15, 17** And the seventh angel blasted a shophar; and there became mega voices in the heavens, wording, The sovereigndoms of this world are become of Yah Veh [3068] {2962}, and of his Mashiyach; and he shall reign into the eons of the eons. Wording, We eucharistize thee, O Yah Veh Elohim Shadday [3068] {2962} [410] {2316} [7706] {3841}, being the being, and the having been, and him the coming being; because thou hast taken to thee thy mega dynamis, and hast reigned.

**Apocalypse 14:3, 4** And they sing the ode of Mosheh the servant of Elohim, and the ode of the Lamb, wording, Mega and marvellous are thy works, Yah Veh Elohim Shadday [3068] {2962} [410] {2316} [7706] {3841}; just and true are thy ways, thou Sovereign of the holy. Who shall never ever awe thee, O [3068] {2962} Yah Veh, and glorify thy name? because thou only art hallowed: because all Goyim shall come and worship in sight of thee; because thy judgments are manifest.

# Names 26

**Apocalypse 14:5** And I heard the angel of the waters wording, Thou art just, O Yah Veh [3068] {2962}, which also being the being, and the having been being, and *shalt be** the hallowed being, because thou hast judged these.

*most mss omit *shalt be*

**Apocalypse 16:7, 8** And I heard another from the sacrifice altar wording, Yes, Yah Veh Elohim Shadday [3068] {2962} [410] {2316} [7706] {3841}, true and just are thy justices. Because of this shall her plagues come in one day, death, and mourning, and famine; and she shall be burned in fire: because forceful is Yah Veh Elohim who judgeth her.

**Apocalypse 19:1** And after these I heard a mega voice of vast throngs in the heavens, wording, Halalu Yah [1984] [3050] {239} ; Salvation, and glory, and honour, and dynamis, unto [3068] {2962} Yah Veh our Elohim:

**Apocalypse 19:6** And I heard as the voice of a vast throng, and as the voice of vast waters, and as the voice of forceful thunderings, wording, Halalu Yah [1984] [3050] {239}: because Yah Veh El Shadday [3068] {2962} [410] {2316} [7706] {3841} reigneth.

**Apocalypse 21:22** And I saw no holy of holies in it: indeed Yah Veh Elohim Shadday [3068] {2962} [410] {2316} [7706] {3841} and the Lamb being the holy of holies of it.

**Apocalypse 22:5, 6** And there shall be no night there; and they have no need of candle. neither also light of the sun; because [3068] {2962} [430] {2316} Yah Veh Elohim illuminateth them: and they shall reign into the eons of the eons.

And he said unto me, These words *are* trustworthy and true: and [3068] {2962} [430] {2316} Yah Veh Elohim of the holy prophets apostolized his angel to shew unto his servants those that must become in quickness.

# 27 Panoramas of

## PANORAMA OF THE NAME OF THE SAVIOUR

The Proverb of Lemu El:

Who ascended to the heavens

— or descended?

Who gathered the wind in his fists?

Who narrowed the waters in a cloth?

Who raised all the finalities of the earth?

What is his name?

What is the name of his son

— if you know?

Proverbs 30:4

## THE MISNOMER OF THE NAME OF THE SAVIOUR

An expression often repeated
often becomes believable.

"The 'Greeks' had a word for it"
is one of the most infamous.

And 'Greek' is the misnomer for 'Hellene', the tongue of most of the first century translations of the New Covenant.

The Greek mistranslation of the name of the Saviour is {2424} Iesous. As the 'Greek' alphabet has no **Y**, they substituted **IE** for the mistranslation of **Yah** — the Eternal Being of the Old Covenant.

And worst of all, they substituted the name of the Greek God **{2203} Zeus** as the suffix.

So **Ie Zeus** translates to **Eternal Zeus.**

Let me tell you, my dear friend, that is **not** the name of my Saviour.

And then the intelligencia has mistranslated the Greek mistranslation even further with the name, **JESUS**.

# Names 28

**PRIMA FACIA EVIDENCE OF THE NAME:**

Fortunately, there is **evidence — absolutely positive evidence** — over which there no shadow of doubt of his name:

- {2424} **iesous** of Hebrew origin [3091].

And the Hebrew origin:

- [3091] **Yehowshua** — which is a compounding of:
- [3068] **Yehovah**; Eternal:and
- [3167] **yasha**; Salvation.

Other scholars trace the name to:

- [3050] *Yahh* **Yah** Eternal
- [8668] *teshuah* **Shua** Salvation.

And this single verse gives us, not only the name, but the reason and definition of the name.

**Matthaios 1:21**

. . . thou shalt call his name Yah Shua: for he shall save his people from their sins.

In other words:

Thou shalt call his name Eternal Saviour: for he shall save his people from their sins.

**AND HIS NAME SHALL BE CALLED:**

**Yesha Yah 7:14** Therefore Adonay himself shall give you a sign; Behold! A virgin shall conceive, and birth a son, and shall call his name **Immanu El***.

*El with us

**Yesha Yah 9:6** And his name (singular) shall be called, Marvellous — Counsellor — Mighty El — Eternal Father — Governor of Shalom.

**THE SELF—HUMBLING OF HA MASHIYACH**

**Philippians 2:5—8** Indeed, Let this mind be in you, which was also in ha Mashiyach Yah Shua: Who, existing in the form of Elohim, deemed it not usurption to be equal with Elohim: But voided himself, and took upon him the form of a servant, and became in the likeness of humanity: And being perceived in configuration as a human, he humbled himself, and became obedient until death, even the death of the stake.

**THE EXALTATION OF HA MASHIYACH**

**Philippians 2:9—11** Therefore Elohim also hath most highly exalted him, and graced him a name which is above every name: So that in the name of Yah Shua every knee should bow, in the heavenlies, and in the earthly, and the subterranean;

And that every tongue should avow that Yah Shua ha Mashiyach is Adonay, unto the glory of Elohim the Father

# 29 Panoramas of

## TRIUNE HUMANITY

**1 Thessalonians 5:23**

And the Elohim of Shalom himself hallow you in shalom, and guard your whole **spirit** and **soul** and **body** blameless in the parousia of our Adonay Yah Shua ha Mashiyach.

**physiology** *noun* the study of the body.

**body** *noun* the physique of the being.

**1 Corinthians 15:44—46**

We also have a **soulical body** and a **spiritual body.**

While on earth, **the physical body** is the house of the **soulical body** and the **spiritual body**.

### BREATHING

The appetites of the physical being are expressed by the rapid inhalation and exhalation breath — also known as, "the panting of the flesh."

## THE BODY OF THE SAVIOUR: AS THE ETERNAL WORD

**Yah Chanan 1:1—5** In the begining, the Word having been,And the Word having been unto Elohim, and Elohim having been the Word, he having been in the beginning unto Elohim; All became through his hand, and without him, not even one being whatever became. In him, life became — the life having the light of the son of humanity: and the light enlightened the darkness, and the darkness overtook it not.

**Yah Chanan 1:14** And the Word, being flesh, and resting within us, and we, seeing his glory — the glory as of the only birthed of the Father, filled with grace and truth.

From the Aramaic

## AS THE BODY OF THE CREATOR

**Colossians 1:16, 19** And by him all was created — in the heavens and on the earth — all that is seen and all that is not seen.

— that in him, all fullness willed to inhabit.

**Colossians 2:9** In whom inhabits all the fullness of Deity bodily.

# Physiology 30

## BODY OF HUMANITY AND THE SAVIOUR

**Psalm 8:1—6**

To His Eminence upon Gittith,
A Psalm of David.
O Yah Veh our adoni,
how mighty is thy name in all the earth!
who hast given thy grandeur above the heavens.
From the mouth of sucklings and sucklers
hast thou founded strength
because of thine tribulators,
that thou shabbathizest
the enemy and the avenger.
When I see thy heavens,
the work of thy digits,
the moon and the stars,
which thou hast established;
What is a mortal*,
that thou rememberest him?
and the son of humanity**,
that thou visitest him?
For thou hast made him a bit lacking Elohim,
and hast crowned him with glory and majesty.
Thou hast him to rule
over the works of thy hands;
thou hast set all under his feet:

*human mortal:
**Yah Shua, the son of humanity

## THIS BODY OF FLESH — A BASKET CASE

**Galatians 5:17** Indeed the flesh panteth against the Spirit.

**Romans 7:18** Indeed I know that in me (that is, in my flesh,) dwelleth no good: indeed to will is present with me; but to work that which is good I perceive not.

**1 Petros 4:1, 2** then as ha Mashiyach hath suffered for us in flesh, equip yourselves likewise with the same mind: because he that hath suffered in flesh hath paused from sin; Unto his never again existing his remaining time in flesh according to the pantings of humanity, but to the will of Elohim.

### SNEAK PREVIEW

**Romans 3:16, 17** Know see ye not that ye are the holy of holies of Elohim, and the Spirit of Elohim dwelleth in you? If any defile the holy of holies of Elohim, him shall Elohim defile; Indeed the holy of holies of Elohim is holy, which ye are.

**1 Corinthians 6:19** Or see ye not that your body is the holy of holies of the Holy Spirit in you, which ye have from Elohim, and ye are not your own?

# 31 Panoramas of

## PANORAMA OF PSYCHOLOGY
## TRIUNE HUMANITY

**1 Thessalonians 5:23**

And the Elohim of Shalom himself hallow you in shalom, and guard your whole **spirit** and **soul** and **body** blameless in the parousia of our Adonay Yah Shua ha Mashiyach.

**1 Corinthians 15:44**

...There is a **soulical body.**

**Psychology** *noun* the study of the soul.

•[5315] **nephesh** *noun* soul, the seat of the emotions.

•{5590} **psuche** *noun* English, **psyche, soul.**

**Genesis 2:7** And Yah Veh Elohim formed adam/humanity of the dust of the soil, and breathed into his nostrils the breath of life; and adam/humanity became a living soul.

## BREATHING

The appetites of the soulical being are expressed by the inhalation of breath. The inhalation of breath feeds oxygen to the blood.

## THE SOUL OF THE FLESH IS IN THE BLOOD

**Leviticus 17:11—14** For the soul of the flesh is in the blood: and I have given it to you upon the sacrifice altar to kaphar/atone for your souls: for it is the blood that kaphar/atoneth for the soul. Therefore I said unto the sons of Yisra El, No soul of you shall eat blood, neither shall any sojourner that sojourneth among you eat blood. And man — any man of the sons of Yisra El, or of the sojourners that sojourn among you, which hunteth a hunt of any live being or flyer that may be eaten; he shall even pour out the blood thereof, and cover it with dust.. For it is the soul of all flesh; the blood of it is for the soul thereof: therefore I said unto the sons of Yisra El, Ye shall eat the blood of no flesh: for the soul of all flesh is the blood thereof: whosoever eateth it shall be cut off.

**THE SOUL**
**IS THE SUSTAINER OF LIFE.**

And speaking of BREATHING,

## TIME OUT FOR A BREATHER

When I was a lad of 65, in my search for a deeper spiritual life, I asked myself a question, "What's the difference between **soul** and **spirit**?"

And in my research I discovered that **soul** was mistranslated into more than forty different words.

Then I asked myself a question that altered the course of my whole life . . .

What would happen if I researched every word of Scripture — 8,600 Hebraic and Aramaic, and 5,500 Heleenic and Aramaic — more than 14,000 words?

Ten years later, on my 75th birthday, my first exeGeses Ready Research Bible was accepted for publishing. And to this day, exeGeses Bibles (uncluding the Aramaic new Covenant) are the only Literal Translations & Transliterations of Scripture.

May I encourage you, Dear Friend, that whenever the Holy Spirit gives you a holy hunch, that you follow through. It just may be that you have been selected to alter the course of the aeons.

## SOUL IS THE THRONE OF THE EMOTIONS

The soul
bereaves,
blesses,
craves,
embitters,
grieves,
halals,
hates,
hopes,
loaths,
longs,
loves,
rejoices,
yearns.

The soul
lives,
dies,
resurrects.

# 33 Panoramas of

## AN IN DEPTH STUDY OF THE SOUL ADAPTED FROM THE LEXICON OF THE EXEGESES PARALLEL BIBLE

**SOUL, SOULICAL, SOULLESS:**

**soul** *noun* nephesh [5315] psuchee {5590} the psyche; the soul is the center of the emotional attributes; the soul of the flesh is in the blood; **read** Leviticus 17:11; the inhalation of breath brings oxygen to the blood, which brings life to the flesh; the soul sustains life, but is not life itself; Yah Veh puffed (ex—souled) (ex—haled) into the nostrils of Adam; and Adam became a living soul; **see** puff; **read** Genesis 2:7; all living beings have souls; **note:** most versions render the Hebrew and Aramaic word nephesh into more than forty differents words, and the Hellene word psuchee (psyche) into seven different words; only soul is correct; **cp** spirit.

**soulical** *adjective* psuchikos {5591} emotional.

**soulless** *noun* apsuchos {895} without soul; figuratively, without emotion.

**doublesouled** *adjective* dipsukos {1374} in the sense of being two—faced.

# Physiology 34

**likesouled** *noun* isopsuchos {2473} with similar emotions.
**timidsouled** *adjective* oligopsukos {3642} shy of soul.
**well–souled** *adjective* eupsucheo {2174} of beneficient soul.
**expire** *verb* gava [1478] to breathe one's last breath.
**expire soul** *verb* naphach [5301] ekpsucho {1634} to puff away one's soul; to pressure, as in a pressure cooker.
**puffed up** *adjective* phusioo {5448} as soulical pride.
**puffings up** *noun* phusiosis {5450} soulically proud.
**puff** *verb* naphach [5301] emphusao {1720} to blow hard; from nephesh; the Septuagint translates the Hebraic naphach to the Hellenic emphuzao; this word is used of Yah Veh puffing into Adam; of the Holy Spirit puffing into the dry bones; and of Yah Shua puffing into the disciples.
**puff** *verb* nasham [5395[ nashaph [5398[ to blow away; from nephesh.

# 35 Panoramas of

## THE SOUL AND SHEOL:

- [7585] **sheol** *noun* abode of the dead.
- {86} **hades** *noun* unseen; abode of the dead.

Theologians of all theories vary widely on the subject of **sheol**. I beseech that we not schism and frustrate our blessing.

### SHEOL HAS A SOUL:

**Yesha Yah 5:14** Therefore sheol hath broadened her soul, and opened her mouth without statute: and their majesty, and their multitude, and their roaring, and he that jumpeth for joy, shall descend into it.

**Hoshea 13:14** I shall ransom them from the hand of sheol; I shall redeem them from death: O death, I shall be thy pestilence; O sheol, I shall be thy destruction: repentance shall be hid from mine eyes.

**1 Corinthians 15:55, 56** O death, where thy sting? O sheol, where thy triumph? But the sting of death is sin; but the dynamis of sin is the torah.

## PROPHECY OF DAVID CONCERNING THE SOUL OF YAH SHUA HA MASHIYACH:

**Psalm 16:10** For thou shalt not forsake my soul in sheol; neither shalt thou give thy mercied to see the pit of ruin.

**Acts 2:27—31** Because thou shalt not leave my soul in sheol, nor even shalt thou give thine hallowed to see corruption. Thou hast notified to me the ways of life ; thou shalt fill me with joy with thy face. Men, brethren, allow me with boldness to say unto you concerning the patriarch David, that he hath also died and is entombed, and his tomb is among us unto this day. Therefore being a prophet, and knowing that Elohim had oathed an oath to him, that of the fruit of his loins, according to the flesh, he should raise ha Mashiyach to be seated upon his throne; He foreseeing this spake concerning the resurrection of ha Mashiyach, that his soul was not left in sheol, nor even his flesh did see corruption.

# Psychology 36

## THE MINISTRY OF YAH SHUA IN SHEOL

**1 Petros 3:18,19 as translated from the Hellenic:**

For ha Mashiyach also hath once suffered concerning sins, the just for the unjust, so that he might bring us to Elohim, being deathified indeed in the flesh, but enlivened by the Spirit: In which also he went and preached unto the spirits in prison. . . .

**1 Petros 3:18,19 as translated from the Aramaic:**

Because also ha Mashiyach died one time for our sins — the just for sinners, to offer us to Elohim — and deathified in body and enlivened in Spirit: and preaching to the souls being held in sheol.

Whereas the Hellenic translation has no correlation with any other verse in Scripture, the Aramaic enlightens us as to his ministry while his body was dead.

And when he was resurrected,
**Matthaios 27:52, 53** And the tombs were opened; and many bodies of the holy which slept arose, And departed from the tombs after his resurrection, and entered into the Holy city, and appeared unto many.

## THE SOULS UNDER THE ALTAR

**Apocalypse 6:9—11** And when he had opened the fifth seal, I saw under the sacrifice altar the souls of them that were slaughtered because of the word of Elohim, and because of the witness which they had: And they cried with a mega voice, wording, Until when, O Despotes, holy and true, dost thou not judge and avenge our blood from them that dwell upon the earth?

And white stoles were given unto each; and it was rhetorized unto them, so that they should relax yet a bitty time, until their co—servants also and their brethren, that are about to be slaughtered as also they, should be fulfilled.

### THE AXED SOULS REIGN WITH HA MASHIYACH

**Apocalypse 20:4** And I saw thrones, and they seated upon them, and judgment was given unto them and the souls of them that were beheaded because of the witness of Yah Shua, and for because of the word of Elohim, and which had not worshipped the beast, nor even his icon, also neither had received his tattoo upon their foreheads, also upon their palms; and they lived and reigned with ha Mashiyach a thousand years.

## OLD COVENANT: SPIRIT vs WIND
## TRIUNE HUMANITY

**1 Thessalonians 5:23**
And the Elohim of Shalom himself hallow you in shalom, and guard your whole **spirit** and **soul** and **body** blameless in the parousia of our Adonay Yah Shua ha Mashiyach.

•**pneumatology** *noun* the study of the spirit.

•[7307] **ruwach** *noun* spirit, wind

The **spirit** is the throne of the **mental attributes** — including, but not limited to **memory**, **volition**, **will**, **wisdom**.

## BREATHING: THE PUFF:

The respiration of the spirit is associated with the exhalation of breath.
**Yah Chanan 4:8** The Spirit puffeth where he willeth.
**Yah Chanan 20:22** And when he had said this, he puffed into them, and wordeth unto them, Receive ye the Holy Spirit.

## BREATHING: THE SIGH

**Genesis 6:6** And Yah Veh **sighed** [5162] that he had made humanity.

**Romans 8:26** Then Likewise the Spirit also co—helpeth our frailties: indeed we know not what we should pray for as we need: but the Spirit himself interceedeth for us with **sighings** {4726} unutterable.

## THE PERSON OF THE HOLY SPIRIT

In the Old Covenant, the Spirit of Elohim, is referred to as the **Holy Spirit** only in Psalm 51:11.
In the New Covenant, he is referred to as the **Holy Spirit**, and in some Versions, as the **Holy Ghost**. The term **Ghost** is derived from the Saxons and the Germanic languages. We deeply respect those who would use this term.
In modern English, **ghost** is defined as the spirit of a dead person — and I sense that the Holy Spirit is very much alive.

# Pneumatology 38

## THE MINISTRY OF THE HOLY SPIRIT

The ministry of the Holy Spirit was first evidenced in creation — where the Spirit of Elohim brooded over the face of the waters.

Genesis 1:2

The Holy Spirit became the 'another Paraclete' after the parousia of Yah Shua, to guide us.

Yah Chanan 14:16

The Holy Spirit is our intercessor.

Romans 8:26

The Holy Spirit is the bestower of spirituals.

1 Corinthians 12:11

And Oh so much more!

In the Old Covenant, some Scriptures require great discernment on whether to translate **wind** or **spirit**. When in doubt, the exeGeses Bibles translated thus: spirit/wind.

However there is absolutely no excuse to mistranslate **Spirit** in Yechezq El 37.

## THE VISION OF THE VALLEY OF DRY BONES

**Yechezq El 37:1—6** The hand of Yah Veh became upon me, and got me in the spirit [7307] of Yah Veh, and rested me in the midst of the valley which was full of bones, And caused me to pass by them round about: and, behold, there were exceedingly many at the face of valley; and, Behold, they were exceedingly dry.

And he said unto me, Son of humanity, can these bones live? And I said, O Adonay Yah Veh, thou knowest.

Again he said unto me, Prophesy upon these bones , and say unto them, O ye dry bones, hearken to the word of Yah Veh.

Thus saith Adonay Yah Veh unto these bones; Behold, I shall cause the spirit [7307] to enter you, and ye shall live: And I shall give sinews upon you, and shall ascend flesh upon you, and cover you with skin, and give spirit [7307] in you, and ye shall live; and ye shall know that I am Yah Veh.

## NEW COVENANT: SPIRIT vs WIND

•{4151} **pneuma** *noun* spirit (not wind)
•{317} **anemos** *noun* wind (not spirit)

In the New Covenant, **pneuma** means **spirit**.

Depending on the Bible Version, pneuma is always translated **spirit** or (holy) **Ghost** — except for one verse Yah Chanan (John) 3:8.

Every Bible Version mistranslates pneuma as wind in Yah Chanan 3:8 — except Young's Literal Translation, and the exeGeses Literal Translation and Transliteration.

Here's how the Authorized King James Version mistranslates this verse:

The wind bloweth where it listeth, and thou hearest the sound thereof, but canst not tell whence it cometh, and whither it goeth: so is everyone that is born of the Spirit.

Now compare your Bible Version.

In Yah Chanan 3:1—7 Yah Shua is speaking of the "upper birth" — that it is a spiritual experience — and 3:8 is the summation of 3:1—7.

## A Literal Translation & Transliteration:

## THE SPIRIT BIRTH

**Yah Chanan 3:1—8** There had been a human of the Separatists, named Nikodemos, an archon of the Yah Hudiym: The same came to Yah Shua by night, and said unto him, Rabbi, we know that thou art a Rabbi come from Elohim: for not even any is able to do these signs that thou doest, unless Elohim be with him.

Yah Shua answered and said unto him, Amen, amen, I word unto thee, Unless any be birthed from above, he is not able to see the sovereigndom of Elohim.

Nikodemos wordeth unto him, How is a human able to be birthed being old? is he able to enter twice into his mother's womb, and be birthed?

Yah Shua answered, Amen, amen, I word unto thee, Unless one be birthed of water and Spirit {4151}, he is not able to enter into the sovereigndom of Elohim. That which is birthed of the flesh hath become flesh; and that which is birthed of the Spirit {4151} hath become spirit {4151}. Marvel not that I said unto thee, Ye must be birthed from above.

# Pneumatology 40

The Spirit {4151} puffeth where he willeth, and thou hearest the voice of him, but knowest not whence it cometh and whither it goeth: thus be all that are birthed of the Spirit {4151}.

## THE HUMAN SPIRIT

Within the **human spirit** lies the potential for all achievement. Within this potential, the **human spirit** may decide to stay in bed, become a recluse, or change the world.

Here are a few admonitions to guide you along the way. How you respond is your decision.

**Ephesians 5:18** Be not drunk with wine, wherein there is excess, but be filled with the Spirit.

**Galatians 5:22** But the fruit of the Spirit is love cheer shalom patience kindness goodness trust meekness self—control*.

*all these are one fruit.

## THE 'IN SPIRIT' EXPERIENCE

We hear so much about living, moving, walking in the Spirit — but in so much vaguity that we have not fathomed the concept.

This is a much holier experience — it is living, moving, walking **In Spirit**. Are you able to grasp that sense of holy communion — that oneness with the fullness of Deity?

The first, and quite possibly the only, requisite of having this **In Spirit** experience is having the Holy Spirit within us.

Imagine where this experience may lead you. Yah Chanan had it.

**Apocalypse 4:1, 2** After these I saw, and, Behold! a portal opened in the heavens: and the first voice which I heard was as of a shophar speaking with me; which worded, Ascend hither, andl shall shew thee what must become.

And after these straightway I became in spirit: and, Behold! a throne was set in the heavens, and one seated upon the throne.

Now I ain't promising you anything — but think of the possibilities.

More to come.

# 41 Panoramas of

## AN IN DEPTH STUDY OF THE SPIRITUALS

### Adapted from the Lexicon of the exeGeses parallel Bible

**SPIRIT, SPIRITS, SPIRITUAL, SPIRITUALS:**
**puff, breathe** *verb* puwach [6315[ **cp** spirit ruwach [7307]: pneo {4154} pnoee {4157} to blow hard.
**expire spirit** *verb* ekpneo {1606} to puff away one's spirit.
**respiration, respite** *noun* revach [7305] revachah [7309] the inspiration and expiration; a spiritual respite; a spirit of rest.
**respire, scent** *verb* ravach [7304] ruwach [7306] ruwach is the *verb* of spirit, wind; literally, to breathe gratuitously; to refresh; to sense through the movement of air.
**Spirit, spirit, spirits** *name, noun* ruwach [7307] [7308] pneuma {4151} the Hebrew and Aramaic word ruwach has the twofold meaning of spirit and wind; the Hellene word pneuma has the single meaning of spirit; **cp** wind.

**The Holy Spirit** is that essence of triune Elohim who participated in the creation, and Who conceived the fleshly body of Elohim, Yah Shua ha Mashiyach. The Holy Spirit guides the spiritually unborn to the Mashiyach; **read** Yah Chanan 3:1–8; the Holy Spirit guides the spiritually birthed into all truth; the Holy Spirit is the "another Paraclete" of the Mashiyach; **read** Yah Chanan 15:26, 16:7–11; the Holy Spirit endues Mashiyachans with the spirituals of energies, ministries, and graces; **read** 1 Corinthians 12:1–11. The King James Version sometimes translates Holy Spirit as Holy Ghost; in Saxon languages, their word for spirit is rooted in our word for ghost; in Latin languages, their word for spirit is rooted in our word for spirit; in modern day English, ghost is a dead spirit; Yah Shua became flesh of the living Holy Spirit of Elohim, and thus we translate Holy Spirit throughout.

**The human spirit** is the center of the mental attributes; the will, memory, thought; including, but not limited, to wisdom, knowledge, prophecy. All Mashiyachans are birthed of, and have the Holy Spirit; but not all Mashiyachans are filled with the Holy Spirit; Mashiyachans may also have "in Spirit" experiences; **read** Apocalypse 4:2.

# Pneumatology 42

**demon spirits** are evil spirits which may possess and control the spiritually unborn, and attack the Mashiyachans.
**spiritual** *adjective* pneumatikos {4152} that mental attribute which is beyond that of the physical, or soulical.
**spiritually** *adverb* pneumatikos {4153} in a spiritual manner.
**spirituals** *noun* pneumatikos {4152} the spirituals bestowed upon humanity are often referred to as spiritual gifts; they are, more accurately, spirituals which the Holy Spirit endues as He wills upon whom He wills. The nine spirituals as presented in 1 Corinthians 12:1–11 are:
(**1**) **word of wisdom** *nouns* logos {3056} sophia {4678} the spiritual of the promise of the ability to decide well.
(**2**) **word of knowledge** *nouns* logos {3056} gnosis {1108} the spiritual of the promise of the awareness of facts not necessarily gained through human experience.
(**3**) **trust** *noun* pistis {4102} **note:** trust is a more accurate translation than the usual words, belief and faith; whereas belief and faith imply a directing of the mind, trust implies a total reliance of the being on another; the Hebrew word for trust is rooted in the word, amen.

(**4**) **charismata of healings** *plural nouns* charisma {5486} iama {2386} the spiritual of having the abilities of healings of various ailments.
(**5**) **energizing** *tr verb* **dynamis** *tr noun* energema {1755} dunamis {1411} the spiritual of energizing the ability; of having the energy and the ability.
(**6**) **word of prophecy** *nouns* logos {3056} prophetia {4394} the spiritual of the ability to foretell; foretell is not to be confused with tell forth; **read** 1 Corinthians 12:10 with 2 Petros 1:19–21.
(**7**) **discernments of spirits** *plural nouns* diakrisis {1253} pneuma {4151} the spiritual ability to distinguish species or qualities of spirits; to test the spirits, whether they be of Elohim.
(**8**) **genos/species of tongues** *adjective/noun* genos {1085} glossa {1100} the spiritual of the ability to express in genos/species of tongues other than those acquired through human experience; including foreign and spiritual tongues.
(**9**) **translation of tongues** *nouns* hermeneia {2058} glossa {1100} the ability to hear a tongue or language other than than learned by human experience, and rendering its meaning; **note:** dreams are interpreted; tongues are translated.

## PANORAMA OF THE CHARISMATA

Here's an interesting group of related words from the same root:

•{5463} **chairo** *verb* the cheer, to hail: quite possible the Hellenic equivelant of halal.
•{5483} **charizomai** *verb* to grace.
•{5484} **charin** *preposition* through grace of
•{5485} **charis** *singular noun*, **charismata** *plural noun* spiritual grace, or graces: the divine influence upon the heart, and its reflection in the life.
•{5486} **charisma** *noun* a spiritual endowment.
•{5487} **charitoo** *verb* to grace.

**1 Corinthians 12:4** Now there are distinctions of **charismata** {5485}, but the same Spirit.

## THE CHARISMATA OF HEALINGS

For those who would usurp the throne of Elohim, and boldly declare, "Divine healing is not for today," may I urge utmost caution.

Yaaqov instructed it — yea commanded that the sick call upon the elders of the ecclesia to pray for them, and they shall be healed.

So why aren't the sick healed in every instance? May I suggest that the person who prays for a Divine healing, and doesn't believe it is an affront — yea, a mockery to Elohim.

Exofficio or not, the personal private life of the Elder ought to conform with the principles laid down in Scripture.

The next time some one in need of healing, search you spirit and see whether you have the **charismata of healings**.

# Charismata 44

## THE CHARISMATA OF THE GENUS OF TONGUES

**genos** {1085} genos *noun* species.
**tongues** {1100{ glossa tongues

Here's a shocker! The word **language** does appear in Scripture — neither in the Old Covenant, nor in the New Covenant. Scripture speaks of **lips**, **tongues**, and **dialects**.

**Genesis 11:9** Yah Veh confounded their **lip**.

**Yesha Yah 28:11** . . . jeering lips and another tongue . . .

**1 Corinthians 14:2** Some versions mention 'unknown tongue'. 'unknown tongue' is unknown in Scripture.

**1 Corinthians 14:21** In the torah it is scribed, in other tongues and other lips shall I speak to this people.

**Tongues** is not a jabbering of the lips that one psyches up.

**Tongues** may be pseudo, of the flesh, or even demonic. Discern!

**Tongues** may also be a Divine Apocalypse (Unveiling) for a certain people at a certain time.

**Tongues** is a **spiritual charismata** bestowed on an **In Spirit** person, understood only by Divine Apocaplypse.

**NOTE:** Whenever you hear someone speaking in tongues, don't peek to see who it is. Merely close your eyes and ask for Divine Discernment.

**Acts 2:1—6** On the day of Pentecost, they were filled full with the Holy Spirit, and tongues of fire sat upon each of them; and they began to speak with other tongues, and the people heard them speak in their own **dialect**.

## THE CHARISMATA OF THE TRANSLATION OF TONGUES

**1 Corinthians 14:13** Wherefore let him that speaketh in a tongue pray so that he may translate.
**1 Corinthians 14:27, 28** If any speak in a tongue, let it be through two, or at the very most three, and that by allotment; and let one translate. But if ye may have no translator, let him hush in the ecclesia; then let him speak to himself , and to Elohim.

The next time you hear someone speaking in tongues, seek discernment, and you may be the person Elohim has selected to unveil the message to the ecclesia. You just never know — until you've obeyed.

# 45 Panoramas of

## ENERGIZING DYNAMIS

Energizing is a transliteration of the Hellenic, energema.

Dynamis is a transliteration of the Hellenic, dynamis.

So what we have here is the fuel and the equipment to accomplish spiritual feats as required.

We have all heard of people who have achieved physical accomplishments beyond the natural in times of stress.

Think ye that Elohim would do less for his holy in time of need?

## TRUST *verb*, TRUST *noun*.

Some people say, **believe** *verb*, and **faith** *noun*. And while this is my opinion, I know I'm right.

While **believe** may be used to imply ones **belief**, it may also be used to imply **doubt**.

Its an old story, but let me retell it. A couple visited a refinery; and on a tour the guide said, "Let me place a globule of molten lead in your palm, and it will roll off and not burn you. Do you believe me?" And the couple said they believed.

When he asked the man to come forward to demonstrate, he said, "Not on your life."

When he asked the woman, she agreed.

Then the guide said, "They both believed, but the woman trusted."

## TRUST IS AN ENERGIZING DYNAMIC

**TRUST** can move mountains. And in modern religious parlance, **faith** has come to mean a **belief system** that one needs to **psyche up**. Think of all the **faith seminars** to seek to build (?) your **faith**.

**TRUST** is dumping your need in someone else's lap. Its no longer your problem.

# Energizings 46

## DISCERNMENTS OF SPIRITS

**Distrusting Spirits:**

**1 Timo Theos 4:1** But the Spirit wordeth rhetorically, that in the latter seasons some shall defect from the trust, heeding to imposter spirits [7307] {4151}, and doctrines of demons {1140};
**1 Yah Chanan 4:3** And every spirit not professing that Yah Shua ha Mashiyach is come in the flesh is not of Elohim . . .
**Apocalypse 16:14** Indeed they are the spirits [7307] {4151} of demons {1142}, doing signs, that proceed upon the sovereigns of the earth and of the whole world, to gather them unto the war of that mega day of Elohim Shadday.

**demon** [7700] **sheg** *noun* demon
**demon** {1140} **daheemon** *noun* demon
**Diabolos** {1228} **deeabolos** *noun*
**Satan** [7854] **satan** *noun* accuser
**Satan** {4567} **satanas** *noun* of Aramaic origin.

Demonic, diabolic, and Satanic spirits may seem like real nice guys (or gals), religious leaders. For Satan is able to transform himself into an angel of light.

2 Corinthians 11:14

## DISCERNMENTS OF SPIRITS

Now that you know a little of what evil spirits are, and how they came and appear to us, let's discuss how we may be able to **distinguish** them.

1. Sometimes you can spot them right off the top — they admit to being the evil spirits they appear to be.

2. Some may be wolves in sheep's clothing — reversed color, mitre, crucifix — the whole nine yards. They are 'interfaith' — thy love each other and everyone else — until you mention 'the religious right'.

### HERE'S A SIMPLE DISCERNMENT TEST

If they deny, or even hem and haw, that Yah Veh is the Creator, that Yah Shua is the Saviour, that the Holy Spirit is the Paraclete, abandon your relationship right now, and fellowship **not**.

## PANORAMA OF MINISTRIES

These three Spirituals are all related to the **word**.

- [1696] **dabar** *verb* word.
- [1697] **dabar** *noun* word.
- {3004} **lego** *verb* word.
- {3056} **logos** *noun* word.

In both the Old Covenant and the New Covenant the verb and the noun carry great force.

In the Old Covenant, in what humanity has named, The Ten Commandments, Scripture named them, The Ten Words.

In the New Covenant, our very Saviour is named, The Word.

In both the Old Covenant and the New Covenant, the verb Word expresses the giving of one's word.

When Yah Shua said, "Amen, Amen, I word unto you," he is giving his word.

In the Spirituals of Ministry, **Word** is an emphatic part of that spiritual.

## THE SPIRITUAL OF THE WORD OF WISDOM

**word** {3050} logos *noun*
**wisdom** {4678} sophia; good judgment, wise decisions.

Imagine yourself, not having the facts at hand, and still making a wise decision.

This Word of Wisdom is a Spiritual not necessarily attained through experience.

## THE SPIRITUAL OF THE WORD OF KNOWLEDGE

**Word** {3050} logos *noun*
**Knowledge** {1108} gnosis *noun*; information.

Knowledge is usually attained through experience — whether subliminal in our observation of life, or whether by research.

Please allow me to ramble a bit. In my initial research of every word of Scripture, I would receive what I called, 'holy hunches'. They had no relationship with my training. Then when I researched further, Lo and behold (a Scriptural expression), they were tested and found true.

Its just this simple, any person with this spiritual gets to learn a lot in a very short time.

## THE SPIRITUAL OF THE WORD OF PROPHECY

**Word** {3050} logos *noun*
**Prophecy** {4394} prophetia *noun*;

While the compilation in Corinthians does not state **word of**, Petros does.

**2 Petros 1:19** We have also a more **steadfast** word {3056} of prophecy {4397}; whereunto ye do well that ye heed, as unto a **candle** that shineth in a dark place, until the day dawn, and the day **phospherescence** arise in your hearts.

Beware those theologians who would rob you of this spiritual by saying that this is more a **forth telling** than a **foretelling**.

This is not a right of passage to open a fortune telling parlor.

We are living in a day of cataclysmic events. And it just may be that the Holy Spirit has endowed you with this sure word of prophecy to warn the world of cataclysms to come, and the salvation to rescue all who trust in the Saviour.

# 49 Panoramas of

## SUMMATION
## THE SPIRITUALS OF THE HOLY SPIRIT

### A Literal Translation & Transliteration

**1 Corinthians 12:1—11** Now concerning spirituals, brethren, I will that you not be unknowing. Ye know that ye were Goyim, taken unto these voiceless idols, as ever ye were led. Therefore I notify you, that not even any speaking in the Spirit of Elohim wordeth Yah Shua anathema: and not even any is able to say Yah Shua Adonay, except in the Holy Spirit.

## CHARISMATA, MINISTRIES, AND ENERGIZINGS

Now there are distinctions of **charismata**, but the same Spirit.

And there are distinctions of **ministries**, but the same Adonay.

And there are distinctions of **energizings**, but it is the same Elohim which energizeth all in all.

But the manifestation of the Spirit is given to each to benefit.

## DISTRIBUTIONS OF SPIRITUALS

Indeed to one is given through the Spirit the **word of wisdom**;

Then to another the **word of knowledge** through the same Spirit;

Then to another **trust** in the same Spirit;

Then to another the **charismata of healings** in the same Spirit;

Then To another the **energizing of dynamis**;

Then to another **prophecy**;

Then to another **discernments of spirits**;

Then to another **genus of tongues**;

Then to another the **translation of tongues**:

## THE HOLY SPIRIT DECIDES WHO GETS WHAT

But all these energizeth that one and the selfsame Spirit, distributing to each in their personal privacy exactly as he has willed.

Now we're getting serious about our Spiritual life. May I suggest that you reread and rereread the forgoing Chapter, red—lining what you sense are the key words. And then rerereread it again.

# Spirituals 50

## CONCLUSION OR A NEW BEGINNING

Allow me a few personal comments.

We who love Yah Veh and seek His holy will are being attacked from without and within.

The world without scoffingly calls us the extreme religious right,

And believers within call us fanatic.

Especially disturbing is the attack on the Holy Scriptures.

Those intellectuals who bring us all these new Bible Versions know the Name. Why do they mistranslate?

To those theologians who misappropriate 1 Corinthians 13:9 in their attempt to invalidate the Spirituals of 1 Corinthians 12: and 14:, allow me to ask, Why then is 13:9 placed between 12: and 14:?

I say their reward (or the lack thereof) cometh.

## LET US PRESS ON!

This teaching is based on Holy Scripture, and is non—contradictable.

As you incorporate 1 Corinthians 12: into your life, being ever mindful of 12:11, ask Yah Veh the Father, Yah Shua the Son, and Ruwach the Spirit to grab hold of your life, and seek the fullness of all the treasures being treasured for you.

## ADMONITIONS

Remember there are always a few pseudos out there with their super spiritual stance — always eager to demonstrate and remonstrate on how to get "that gift".

Then there are the "worship leaders" (we used to call them musicians) — blasting their amplifiers.

"You can't jump start the Holy Spirit,
but you can short circuit His flow."

Don't throw out the Spirituals with the bath water — there is the genuine experience

May you receive them.

# 51 Panoramas of

## PANORAMA OF ANGELS

The Irreligious Left is virtually obsessed with angels — from hoping for an encounter, to the collection of figurines.

And Bible Version mistranslations have hindered our understanding of who they are, and their importance in ministry.

**angel** [4397] Hebraic: malak : messenger
**angel** [4398] Aramaic: malak: messenger
**angel** {32} Hellenic: aggelos: messenger

## ANGEL OF YAH VEH

The first appearance of an angel in the Old Covenant is the ANGEL OF YAH VEH to Hagar in Genesis 16:.

The first appearance of an angel in the New Covenant is the ANGEL OF YAH VEH to Joseph in Matthaios 1:20.

In both references the angel evangelized an evangelism.

## FOOD FOR THOUGHT

The Angel of Yah Veh is often referred to as Theophany — Yah Veh or Yah Shua in physical manifestation.

## ANGELS:
## Who they are, and what they do:

**Psalm 104:4** Who worketh his angels spirits; his ministers unto a flaming fire:,

**Hebrews 1:7** And indeed unto the angels he wordeth, Who maketh his angels spirits, and his ministers a flame of fire.

**Hebrews 1:14** Are they not indeed all ministering spirits, apostolized to minister to them who are about to be heirs of salvation?

**NOTE:** Though angels are ministering spirits, does not mean they are disembodied. All humanity and Deity are body, soul, and spirit.

**Malachi 3:1** Behold, I shall send my angel [4397], and he shall prepare the way at my face: and the adoni, whom ye seek, shall suddenly enter his temple, even the angel [4397] of the covenant, in whom ye are pleased: behold, he shall enter, saith Yah Veh Zaba'aoth.

**Matthaios 11:10** Indeed this is he, concerning whom it is scribed, Behold! I apostolize my angel {32} before thy face, which shall prepare thy way in front of thee.

# Angels 52

**ANGEL RELATED WORDS**

•{31} **angelia** *noun* evangelism

**1 Yah Chanan 3:11** Because this is the evangelism {31} that ye heard from the beginning, so that we should love each other.

•{32} **angelos** *noun* angel

**2 Corinthians 11:14** And no marvel; indeed Satan himself is transfigured into an angel {32} of light.

**2 Corinthians 12:7** And lest I should be superciliously exalted through the pre—eminence of the apocalypses/unveilings {602}, there was given to me a thorn in the flesh , the angel {32} of Satan so as to punch me, lest I should be superciliously exalted.

**Apocalypse 12:7** And there became war in the heavens: Micha El and his angels {32} warred against the dragon; and the dragon warred and his angels {32}, 8 And was not able; nor even was their place perceived yet in the heavens.

•{312} **exangelo** *verb* evangelize,
•{1860} **epangelia** *noun* pre—evangelism

**1 Yah Chanan 1:5** This then also is the pre—evangelism {1860} which we have heard of him, and evangelize {312} unto you, that Elohim is light, and in him is no darkness — not even any.

•{518} **apangelo** *verb* evangelize
8
**Hebrews 2:12** . . . I shall evangelize {518} thy name unto my brethren, in the midst of the congregation/ecclesia shall I hymn unto thee.
Psalm 22:22

•{743} **archangelos** *noun* archangel.

**1 Thessalonians 4:13—16** But I will not have you to be unknowing, brethren, concerning them which sleep, that ye sorrow not, even exactly as the rest which have no hope. Indeed if we trust that Yah Shua died and rose, even thus them also which sleep because of Yah Shua shall Elohim bring united with him. Indeed this we word unto you in the word of Adonay, that we which are living and surviving unto the parousia of Adonay shall not ever precede them which sleep. Because Adonay himself shall descend from the heavens in a summons, in the voice of the archangel, and in the shophar of Elohim: and the dead in ha Mashiyach shall rise firstly:

# 53 Panoramas of

•{53} {1229} **diangello** *verb* evangelize thoroughly

**Romans 9:17** Indeed the scripture wordeth unto Pharaoh, Even that unto this same have I raised thee, that I might indicate my dynamis in thee, and that my name might be evangelized {1229} throughout in all the earth.

•{1804} **exangello** *verb* evangelize

**1 Petros 2:9** But ye are a select genus, a sovereign priesthood, an Holy Goyim, unto being an acquired people; that ye should evangelize {1804} the virtues of him who hath called you from darkness into his marvellous light:

•{1860} **epangelia** *noun* evangelism
•{1861} **epangello** *verb* evangelize

**1 Yah Chanan 2:25** And this is the pre—evangelism {1860} that he hath pre—evangelized {1861} us, life into the eons.

•{2097} **euangello** *verb* evangelize

**Romans 10:15** But how shall they herald, unless they be apostolized? exactly as it is scribed, How beautiful are the feet of them that evangelize {2097} of Shalom, and evangelize {2097} of good!

•{2098} **euangelion** *noun* evangelism,

**Romans 10:16** But they have not all hearkened to the evangelism {2098}. Indeed Yesha Yah wordeth, Adonay, who hath trusted our hearing?

•{2099} **uangelistees** *noun* evangelist

**Acts 21:8** Then on the morrow we that were concerned about Paulos' departed, and came into Kaisaria: and we entered into the house of Philippos the evangelist {2099}, being of the seven; and abode by him.

# Angels 54

## THE FOURFOLD MINISTRY

**Ephesians 4:11** And he gave some indeed, apostles; then, prophets; then evangelists {2099}; then tenders and doctors/rabbis;

**2 Timo Theos 4:5** But be thou sober in all, endure hardship, do the work of an evangelist {2099}, fully bear thy ministry.

•{2465} **isangelos** *adjective* angelic, equal to angels

**Loukas 20:35, 36** But they which shall be accounted worthy to obtain that eon, and the resurrection from the dead, neither even marry, nor even are married off: nor even indeed are they able to die yet: indeed they are equal unto the angels {2465}; and are the sons of Elohim, being the sons of the resurrection.

•{2605} **katangello** *verb* evangelize

**1 Corinthians 9:14** Even thus hath Adonay ordained that they which evangelize {2605} the evangelism {2098} should live of the evangelism {2098}.

•{3853} **parangello** *verb* evangelize

**Acts 10:42** And he evangelized {3853} us to herald unto the people, and to thoroughly witness that it is he which was decreed through Elohim to be the Judge of living and dead{3498}.

**NOTE:** The Hellenic has several verbs — each indicating a slightly different emphasis. {1229} for example, is to evangelize thoroughly.

Only exeGeses Bibles literally translate and transliterate all the words related to angel.

# 55 Panoramas of

## CHERUB, CHERUBIM

•[3742] **kerub** *singular noun* a special order of beings. Cherubim have both animate and inanimate form. Cherubim are beings in various ministries — from guarding in the garden, and as figurines on the atonement cover.

### Cherubim within the Garden

**Genesis 3:24** So he expelled Adam; and he tabernacled Cherubim [3742] at the east of the garden of Eden, and a flaming sword which turned every way, to guard the way of the tree of life.

### Description of the Inanimate Cherubim

as elaborate figurines on the kapporeth/atonement covering.

**Exodus 25:18—22** And thou shalt work two cherubim [3742] of gold, of spinnings shalt thou work them, in the two ends of the kapporeth/atonement covering. And work one cherub [3742] on the one end, and the one cherub [3742] on the other end: even of the kapporeth/atonement covering shall ye work the cherubim [3742] on the two ends thereof.

And the cherubim [3742] shall extend their wings on high, covering the kapporeth/atonement covering with their wings, and their faces shall look man to brother; toward the kapporeth/atonement covering shall the faces of the cherubim [3742] be.

# Cherubim 56

And thou shalt give the kapporeth/atonement covering above upon the ark; and in the ark thou shalt give the witness that I shall give thee. And there I shall congregate with thee, and I shall word with thee from above the kapporeth/atonement covering, from between the two cherubim [3742] which are upon the ark of the witness, of all which I shall mizvah unto the sons of Yisra El.

**Exodus 26:1** Moreover thou shalt work the tabernacle with ten curtains of fine twined bleached linen, and blue, and purple, and scarlet crimson: with cherubim [3742] of fabricated work shalt thou work them.

**The Cherubim as Worked into the Veil**

**Exodus 26:31** And thou shalt work a veil of blue, and purple, and scarlet crimson, and fine twined bleached linen of fabricated work: with cherubim [3742] shall it be worked:

**Exodus 37:7—9** And he worked two cherubim [3742] of gold, of spinnings worked he them, on the two ends of the kapporeth/atonement covering;
8 One cherub [3742] on the end on this side, and one cherub [3742] on the end on that side: out of the kapporeth/atonement covering worked he the cherubim [3742] on the two ends thereof.

And the cherubim [3742] extended their wings on high, and covered with their wings over the kapporeth/atonement covering, with their faces man to brother; even to the kapporeth/atonement covering were the faces of the cherubim [3742].

**Cherubim within the Lectern**

**1 Sovereigns 6:23—32** And within the lectern he worked two cherubim [3742] of olive tree, each ten cubits high. And five cubits was the one wing of the cherub [3742], and five cubits the second wing of the cherub [3742]: from end of the one wing unto the end of the other wing were ten cubits. And the second cherub [3742] was ten cubits: the two cherubim [3742] were of one measure and one shape.

The height of the one cherub [3742] was ten cubits, and so was it of the second cherub [3742].

And he gave the cherubim [3742] midst the inner house: and they extended the wings of the cherubim [3742], so that the wing of the one touched the wall, and the wing of the second cherub [3742] touched the second wall; and their wings touched wing to wing in the midst of the house.

# 57 Panoramas of

**Cherubim within the House**

And he overlaid the cherubim [3742] with gold. And he carved all the walls of the house round about with engraved carvings of cherubim [3742] and palm trees and glistening blossoms, within and without.

And the floor of the house he overlaid with gold, within and without.

**Cherubim on the Doors of the Portal**

And for the portal of the lectern he worked doors of olive tree: the pilaster and side posts were a fifth of the wall.

The two doors also were of olive tree; and he carved upon them carvings of cherubim [3742] and palm trees and glistening blossoms, and overlaid them with gold, and spread gold upon the cherubim [3742], and upon the palm trees.

**Cherubim as Living Beings**

**Psalm 18:10** And he rode upon a cherub [3742], and did fly: yea, he did fly upon the wings of the wind.

**Psalm 80:1** Hear, O Tender of Yisra El, thou that drivest Yoseph like a flock; thou that settlest between the cherubim [3742], shine.

**Psalm 99:1** Yah Veh reigneth; let the people quiver: he settleth between the cherubim [3742]; let the earth quake.

**Yesha Yah 37:16** O Yah Veh Zaba'aoth, Elohim of Yisra El, that settlest between the cherubim [3742], thou art the Elohim, even thou alone, of all the sovereigndoms of the earth: thou hast worked the heavens and earth.

**Yechezq El 9:3** And the glory of the Elohim of Yisra El ascended from the cherub [3742] , whereupon he was, to the threshold of the house. And he called to the man enrobed with linen, which had the scribe's inkhorn by his side;

**THE GLORY OF YAH VEH FILLS THE HOUSE**

**Yechezq El 10:1—9, 14—22** Then I saw, and, behold, in the expanse that was above the head of the cherubim [3742] there was seen over them as a sapphire stone, as the visage of the likeness of a throne.

And he said unto the man enrobed with linen, and said, Enter between the wheels, even under the cherub [3742], and fill thy fist with embers of fire from between the cherubim [3742], and sprinkle them over the city. And he entered in my eye sight.

# Cherubim 58

Now the cherubim [3742] stayed at the right of the house, when the man entered; and the cloud filled the inner court.

Then the glory of Yah Veh lofted from the cherub [3742], and over the threshold of the house; and the house was filled with the cloud, and the court was full of the brilliance of the Yah Veh's glory. And the voice of the cherubim's[3742] wings was heralded even to the outer court, as the voice of El Shadday when he wordeth.

And it became, that when he had mizvahed the man enrobed with linen, saying, Take fire from between the wheels, from between the cherubim [3742]; then he entered, and stayed beside the wheels.

And a cherub [3742] sent his hand from between the cherubim [3742] unto the fire that was between the cherubim [3742], and lifted thereof, and gave it into the fists of him that was enrobed with linen: who took it, and went.

And there was seen in the cherubim [3742] the pattern of a human hand under their wings.

**The Wheel Midst a Wheel**

And I saw, and behold, the four wheels beside the cherubim [3742], one wheel beside one cherub [3742], and one wheel beside one cherub [3742]: and the visage of the wheels was as the eye of a beryl stone.

And each one had four faces: the one face was the face of a cherub [3742], and the second face was the face of a human, and the third the face of a lion, and the fourth the face of an eagle.

And the cherubim [3742] were lifted. This is the living being [2416] that I saw by the river of Kebar.

And when the cherubim [3742] walked, the wheels walked beside them: and when the cherubim [3742] lifted their wings to loft from the earth, the wheels also circled not from beside them.

When they stayed, these stayed; and when they were lifted, these lifted themselves also: for the spirit of the living being [2416] was in them.

Then the glory of Yah Veh went from off the threshold of the house, and stayed over the cherubim [3742]. And the cherubim [3742] lifted their wings, and lifted from the earth in my eyes: when they went, the wheels also were along side them, and he stayed at the portal of the east gate of the Yah Veh's house; and the glory of the Elohim of Yisra El was over them above.

# 59 Panoramas of

This is the living being [2416] that I saw under the Elohim of Yisra El by the river of Kebar; and I knew that they were the cherubim [3742].

Each one had four faces, and each one four wings; and the likeness of the hands of a human was under their wings.

And the likeness of their faces was the same faces which I saw by the river of Kebar, their visage and themselves: they walked each man face forward.

### The Two—Fold Prophecy of the Sovereign of Zor, and Satan

**Yechezq El 28:11—15** Moreover the word of the Yah Veh became unto me, saying, Son of humanity, lift a lamentation upon the sovereign of Zor, and say unto him, Thus saith Adonay Yah Veh; Thou sealest the gauge, full of wisdom, and perfect in beauty. Thou hast been in Eden the garden of Elohim; every precious stone was thy covering, the sardius, topaz, and the diamond, the beryl, the onyx, and the jasper, the sapphire, the emerald, and the carbuncle, and gold: the work of thy tambourines and of thy pipes was prepared in thee in the day that thou wast created.

Thou art the overspreading cherub [3742] that hedgeth in; and I have given thee so: thou wast upon the holy mountain of Elohim; thou hast walked in the midst of the stones of fire. Thou wast integrious in thy ways from the day that thou wast created, till immorality was found in thee.

# Cherubim 60

**Paul, Describing the Tabernacle**

**Hebrews 9:55** Then over it the cherubim [5502] {3742} of glory shadowing the kapporeth/atonement covering; concerning which we are not able now to word according to its allotment.

**Apocalypse 4:6** And in sight of the throne a sea of glass like unto crystaline: and in the midst of the throne, and round about the throne, four living
beings {2226}* full of eyes in front and behind. 7
And the first living being {2226} was like a lion , and the second living being {2226} like a calf, and the third living being {2226} had a face as a human, and the fourth living being {2226} was like a flying
eagle. 8 And the four live beings {2226} had each one throughout them six wings about; And they were full of eyes within: and they have no repose day and night, wording, Holy, holy, holy, Adonay Elohim Shadday, the having been being, and the being being, and the being to come.

*The living beings of the Apocalypse are the same as the cherubim.

And whenever those living beings {2226} give glory and honour and eucharist to him seated upon the throne, who liveth into the eons of the eons, The four and twenty elders fall in sight of him seated upon the throne, and worship him that liveth into the eons the eons of the eons, and cast their wreaths in sight of the throne, wording, Thou art worthy, O Yah Veh, to receive glory and honour and dynamis: because thou hast created all, and through thy will they are and were created.

## SERAPH, SERAPHIM

• [8314] **saraph** *singular noun* burning, copper. Like the Cherubim, the Seraphim are also animate and inanimate beings with the form of a serpent.

## PANORAMA OF THE SERAPHIM

**Numbers 21:—9** And Yah Veh sent seraph {8314} serpents among the people, and they struck the people; and many people of Yisra El died. Therefore the people entered to Mosheh, and said, We have sinned, for we have worded against the Yah Veh, and against thee; I beseech, intercede unto Yah Veh, that he turn aside the serpents from us. And Mosheh interceded for the people.

And Yah Veh said unto Mosheh, Work thee a seraph {8314}, and place it upon a pole: and it shall become, that every one that is stricken, when he seeth it, shall live.

And Mosheh worked a serpent of copper, and placed it upon a pole, And it became, that if a serpent had stricken any man, when he gazed at the serpent of copper, he lived.

**Deuteronomy 8:15** Who walked thee through that great and awesome wilderness, wherein were seraph {8314} serpents, and scorpions, and thirst, where there was no water; who brought thee water out of the rock of flint;

# Seraphim 62

### The Vision of Yesha Yah

**Yesha Yah 6:1—6** In the year that sovereign Uzzi Yah died I saw Adonay seated upon a throne, high and lifted up, and his train filled full the temple. Above it stayed the seraphim {8314}: each one had six wings; with two he covered his face, and with two he covered his feet, and with two he did fly.

And one called unto another, and said, Holy, holy, holy, is the Yah Veh Zaba'aoth: the whole earth is full of his glory.

And the posts of the vestibule shook at the voice of him that called, and the house was filled with smoke.

Then said I, Woe is me! for I am mute; because I am a man of fouled lips, and I settle in the midst of a people of fouled lips: for mine eyes have seen the Sovereign, Yah Veh Zaba'aoth.

Then flew one of the seraphim {8314} unto me, having a live coal in his hand, which he had taken with the tongs from off the sacrifice altar:

**Yesha Yah 14:29** Cheer not thou, all Pelesheth, because the sceptre of him that smote thee is crushed: for out of the serpent's root shall go a hisser, and his fruit shall be a seraph {8314} flying.

### The Burden of the Animals of the South

**Yesha Yah 30:6** The burden of the animals of the south: into the land of tribulation and distress, from whence come the roaring lion and crushing lion, the hisser and flying seraph {8314}, they shall carry lift their valiant upon the shoulders of young asses, and their treasures upon the humps of camels, to a people that shall not benefit them.

**2 Sovereigns 18:4** He turned aside the high bamahs, and crushed the monoliths, and cut the asherim, and crushed the copper [5178] serpent [5175] that Mosheh had worked: for unto those days the sons of Yisra El incensed to it: and he called it Nechustan/Coppery.

**Yah Chanan 3:14—16** And exactly as Mosheh lifted the [8314] {3789} seraph in the wilderness, even thus must the Son of humanity be lifted up: That all trusting in him not destruct, but have life into the eons.

For Elohim loved the world thus, that he gave his only begotten Son that all trusting in him should not destruct, but have life into the eons.

## VIGNETTE: LIGHTEN UP, HERBIE!

Having translated & transliterated Scripture for seventeen years, my inwards churn when I observe some of the fiction and non—fiction being published today. That's why it is somewhat difficult for me to lighten up. But I'll give it my best effort.

Having said all that to say this: Here I go following in their steps — but hopefully with a more Scriptural, yet satisfying (to you and to Elohim) result.

You don't have to be smart to answer this first question correctly — just old (or, is it mature?).

Remember the book — and the seminars, "How to Win Friends and Influence People"?

The book sold by the millions, and the seminars were attended by the thousands. And now, a few generations later, who remembers?

And on its heels came, "The Power of Positive Thinking," and "Possibility Thinking" — both built on Scriptural principles.

And now we have all those seminars on Personal Growth, Personal Prosperity, Personality Development. They take the person who feels inferior, and in progressing steps, become assertive, aggressive, assaultive and explosive. This last one is supposed to help a person reach the ability to "get what I want — I deserve it!"

If I told you right now what you and I 'deserve', you might be quite shocked.

And those "do it yourself" programs, where you look at your own eyeballs in the mirror, and you say your name, followed by, "You're great!" — with that Tony the Tiger accent on "Grrrrreeeeeaaaaat!"

And with all the whiling away of the machinations of humanity, the formula has been unveiled in Holy Scripture.

# Friends & Lovers 64

## HOW to HAVE FRIENDS:

A man with friends
shows himself friendly,
and there is a lover
who adheres closer than a brother.
Proverbs 18:24

So what is a friend? A friend is an acquaintance — someone you know on a personal level. I'd much rather have two friends than one enemy. Wouldn't you?

This world is filled with lonely people — some so lonely, they have become unfriendly — even bitter. No one has reached out to them in decades. They have been passed by — by you, and by others.

It may even be you are one of those lonely ones — and you have been passed by.

You are able to break this vicious cycle!

The next time you bump someone with your shopping cart, say, "Excuse me. I guess I need a driver's test."

Do you have a relative in a 'rest' home? Drop in, greet them with a holy kiss, and leave. You'll both be the friendlier for it.

- {25} **agapo** *verb* love
- {26} **agape** *noun* love
- {5368} **phileo** *verb* befriend
- {5384} **philos** *noun* friend

## LOVE vs BEFRIEND

**Yah Chanan 21:15—17**

So when they had dined, Yah Shua wordeth to Shimon Petros, Shimon, of Yonah, lovest {25} thou me more than these?

He wordeth unto him, Yea, Adonay; thou knowest that I befriend {5368} thee.

He wordeth unto him, Graze my lambs.

He wordeth to him again secondly, Shimon, of Yonah, lovest {25} thou me?

He wordeth unto him, Yea, Adonay; thou knowest that I befriend {5368} thee.

He wordeth unto him, Tend my sheep.

He wordeth unto him thirdly, Shimon, of Yonah, befriendest {5368} thou me?

Petros was sorrowed because he said unto him thirdly, Befriendest {5368} thou me? And he said unto him, Adonay, thou knowest all; thou knowest that I befriend {5368} thee. Yah Shua wordeth unto him, Graze my sheep.

# 65 Vignettes of

## The SH'MA

as recited in some Hebrew and Messianic Congregations:

Hear, O Yisra El:
Yah Veh our Elohim is one Yah Veh:
And thou shalt love Yah Veh thy Elohim
with all thine heart, and with all thy soul,
and with all thy might.
And these words, which I mizvah thee this day,
shall be in thine heart:
And thou shalt point them out unto thy sons,
and shalt word of them
when thou settlest in thine house,
and when thou walkest by the way,
and when thou liest, and when thou risest.
And thou shalt bind them
for a sign upon thine hand,
and they shall be as phylacteries between thine eyes.
And thou shalt scribe them
upon the posts of thy house, and on thy gates.

Deuteronomy 6:4—9

**Markos 12:29—33**

Then Yah Shua answered him, That The foremost of all the mizvoth is, Hear, O Yisra El; Yah Veh our Elohim is one Yah Veh: And thou shalt love Yah Veh thy Elohim with all thy heart , and with all thy soul, and with all thy mind, and with all thy strength: this is the foremost mizvah. And the second is like, this is it: Thou shalt love thy neighbour as thyself. There is not another mizvah greater than these.

And the scribe said unto him, Well, Rabbi, thou hast said upon the truth: because there is one Elohim; and there is not another but he: And to love him with all the heart, and with all the comprehension, and with all the soul, and with all the strength, and to love neighbour as self, is more than all holocausts and sacrifices.

## HOW TO GET ALL THE LOVE YOU CAN HANDLE

1. Love Elohim.
2. Love your neighbour as thyself.

Scripture does not teach self—love:
It assumes it.

Whether you are conceited or not, when you love your neighbour as much as you love yourself, your neighbour's love will bounce back. You might even try this on your enemies.

# Friends & Lovers 66

## THE WAY OF LOVE

If ever I speak with the tongues of humanity and of angels,
but have not love,
I am become as echoing copper, or a halooing cymbal.
And If ever I have prophecy,
and know all mysteries,
and all knowledge;
and if ever I have all trust, thus to remove mountains,
but have not love {26},
I am not even aught.
And if ever I force feed all my holdings on others,
and if ever I surrender my body to be burned,
but have not love {26},
it benefitteth me not even aught.
Love {26} is patient, is kind;
love {26} is never jealous;
love {26} never braggeth, never puffs,
Never misbehaveth, never self— seeking,
never agitated, never reckoneth evil;

Never cheereth over injustuce,
but co—rejoiceth in the truth;
Endureth all, trusteth all, hopeth all, abideth all.
Love {26} never ever faileth:
but whether prophecies, they shall inactivate;
whether tongues, they shall pause;
whether knowledge, it shall inactivate.
Indeed we know by allotment, and we prophesy by allotment.
But whenever that shalom hath come,
then that which is by allotment shall be inactivated.
When I was a baby, I spake as a baby,
I minded as a baby, I reckoned as a baby:
but when I became a man, I inactivated the baby.
Indeed now we observe through a mirror, in obscurity;
but then face to face:
now I know by allotment;
but then shall I know exactly as also I am known.
But now abideth trust, hope, love, these three; but the greatest concerning these is love {26}.

1 Corinthians 13:

# 67 Vignettes of

## USED

Ever hear these grand quotes?
"I felt so used!" or, "He used me!"

My, my! Pity, pity!

Whenever a lover bestows a gift on his beloved, the gift is of no value until the beloved uses the gift. If the beloved placed the gift on the shelf, should not the lover be offended?

A car parked in a garage depreciates in value, used or not, abused or not (unless it turns out to be a classic).

You however, the more you are used, the more you appreciate in value. Think on these.

## ABUSED

In the 'good old days' we used to hear,

Train up a child in the way he should go,
and when he is old
he shall not depart from it.

Or as the exeGeses translations says,

Hanukkah a lad by mouth about his way,
and when he has aged
he shall not turn aside from it.

Proverbs 22:6

Here's a good one:

Spare the rod, and spoil the child.

Or, as Scripture scribes:

He that spareth the rod hateth his son:
but he that loveth him,
rising early, disciplineth him.

Proverbs 13:24

Try that today, and they'll take your child away, and stick you in the clinker on charges of child abuse.

Oh I know, and you know there are legitimate charges concerning child abuse.

But I am thinking of couples of high esteem, who adopt abandoned children — couples who devote much of their lives to care for them into adulthood. And after they have passed away, the children earn their own fortunes telling the world how mean their mommies and daddies were.

And then there are the children who were abused, and they have grown into adulthood — men and women of character — genuine assets to society.

All that to say this,

Elohim holds you responsible
for what you do
with what you've got.

# Used, Abused — 68

## BROKEN

**Yirme Yah 18:1—7**

The word which came to Yirme Yah from Yah Veh, saying, Arise, and go descend to the potter's house, and there I shall cause thee to hearken to my words.

Then I descended to the potter's house, and, behold, he worked a work on the stones. And the vessel that he worked of clay was ruined in the hand of the potter: so he worked it, turning another vessel, as was straight in the eyes of the potter to work it.

Then the word of the Yah Veh came to me, saying, O house of Yisra El, Am I not able to work with you as this potter? — an oracle of Yah Veh. Behold, as the clay is in the potter's hand, so are ye in mine hand, O house of Yisra El.

There are times when we think we are seeing ourselves as we are, and in desperation, we give up.

But Elohim sees us as what we are able to be. There are times when he gives us a word of encouragement — there are times when he breaks us, and makes of us a new vessel, able to contain all the glories he has prepared us who love him.

## SHATTERED

**Mark 14:3—6**

And Yah Shua, being in Beth Ania in the house of Shimon the leper, as he reposed, there came a woman having an alabaster of myrrh of nard very precious; and she shattered the alabaster, and poured it on his head.

Now there some were indignant within themselves, and worded, Unto what becometh this destruction of the myrrh? Indeed this was able to have been sold for more than three hundred denarion, and have been given to the poor. And they snorted against her.

Then Yah Shua said, Allow her; why belabour and embarrass ye her? she hath worked a good work unto me.

**Matthaios 26:12**

Indeed in that she hath poured this myrrh over my body, she did it unto my embalmment.

Ever walk through a field of fresh mown hay? Every stalk has been clipped and a myriad of raw edges send forth their sweet smell.

The rose on the vine has a pleasing odor. But not til it is crushed does it share its full fragrance.

## JUSTICE

### JUSTICE IS GETTING WHAT YOU DESERVE

"All I want is my fair share."
"All I want is what's rightfully mine."
"I demand justice!"

Ever hear those words on the lips of another?
Ever utter them from your own mouth?

Careful! You may get what your asking for.
And you may get it withour asking for it.

You — yes you — I mean you have sinned and come short of the glory of Elohim.

Would you, in this state, demand justice? I think not!

## VENGEANCE

### VENGEANCE IS WISHING JUSTICE ON ANOTHER

Vengeance is usually expressed as getting one's rights — I just want to get even.

There is no such thing as 'even'. When you get the best of your neighbour, and gloat over it, your neighbour is 'evener' than you.
Vengeance is a 'self—destruct'.

The only one I know who can handle vengeance is you know who — Elohim.

Think of the shalom you would possess in your inner being if you trusted in the ultimate Victor to gain the victory.

**Romans 12:19**
Beloved, avenge not yourselves, but give place unto wrath: indeed it is scribed, Vengeance is mine; I shall reciprocate, wordeth Yah Veh.

**Deuteronomy 32:35**
Vengeance is mine, and retribution;

## FORGIVENESS

### FORGIVING IS GETTING FORGIVENESS

Now that sounds stupidly simple, does it not? And that's precisely how simple it is.

Is there someone who 'ticks you off' — someone who 'ticked you off' — and you've got this little teeny weeny grudge against them?

Here's whatcha gotta do:

1. Ask Elohim to forgive you;
2. Forgive yourself;
3. This is the tuffy — whether you are right or wrong — makes no difference — ask them to forgive you. Wow! That hurts — but feels so good afterwards.

Here are a few of the possible, probable results:

1. They may not have known of your grudge, and resent you forever.
2. They may have had the same grudge toward you, and admire you for taking the first step

Here is the one positive result:

1. Elohim will have forgiven you.
Time for a little inner cleansing? Go for it!

**Matthaios 6:15**

Indeed If ever ye forgive humanity their backslidings, your heavenly Father shall also forgive you: But unless ye forgive not humanity their backslidings, neither shall your Father forgive your backslidings.

# 71 Vignettes of

## MERCY

### MERCY IS NOT GETTING WHAT YOU DESERVE

**Ephesians 2:1—7**

And you, being dead in backslidings and sins; Wherein which ever ye walked according to the eon concerning this world, according to the archon of the authority of the air, the spirit that now energizeth in the sons of distrust: Among whom also we all had our behavior ever in the pantings of our flesh, doing the will of the flesh and of the mind; and were by nature the children of wrath, even also as the rest: but Elohim, being rich in mercy, through his great vast love wherewith he loved us, Even when we, being dead in backslidings, hath co—enlivened with ha Mashiyach, (by grace ye are saved;) And hath co—raised, and co—seated in the heavenlies in ha Mashiyach Yah Shua: so that in the eons to come he might indicate the exceeding riches of his grace in his kindness upon us in ha Mashiyach Yah Shua.

## GRACE

### GRACE IS GETTING WHAT YOU DON'T DESERVE

**Ephesians 2:8—10**

Indeed by grace are ye saved through trust; and that not of yourselves: it is the qurban of Elohim: Not of works, lest any should boast.

Indeed we are his making, created in ha Mashiyach Yah Shua upon good works, which Elohim hath previously prepared so that we should walk in them.

The **mercy** of Elohim is knit with his **grace**.

No matter how reserved you are, shout **HALLALU YAH!** I mean, really shout!

~ ~ ~

Aramaic, the tongue of the Saviour, and of much of the New Covenant, sheds great light of grace. In what theologians have named The Beatitudes, and have had great difficulty describing the word Blessed, the Aramaic simply says, Graced — the verb of the unmerited and undeserved Grace.

# Mercy — 72

**Matthaios 5:1—12**

Then having seen the throngs, he ascended into a mountain: and when he was seated, his disciples came unto him: And he opened his mouth, and doctrinated them, saying wording,

Graced are the poor in spirit:
because theirs is the sovereigndom of the heavens.

Graced are they that mourn:
because they shall be comforted.

Graced are the meek:
because they shall inherit the earth.

Graced are they which do hunger famish and thirst after justness:
because they shall be filled.

Graced are the merciful:
because they shall be mercied.

Graced are the pure in heart:
because they shall see Elohim.

Graced are they that shalam:
because they shall be called the sons of Elohim.

Graced are they which are pursued for cause of justness: because theirs is the sovereigndom of the heavens.

Graced are ye, when ever ye shall be reviled, and pursued,and shall say all rhema of evil concerning you falsely,because of me.

Cheer, and jump for joy:because vast is your reward in the heavens:indeed thus pursued they the prophets preceding you.

Marvelous, infinite, matchless grace:
Grace that exceeds our sin and our guilt.
Grace that is greater, yes grace untold;
will you this moment his grace receive.
Grave, Grace, Infinite grace:
Grace that will pardon and cleanse within:
Grace, Grace, infinite grace:
Grace that is greater than all our sin.

Please pray with me:

Dear Elohim Yah Veh, in the name of your son Yah Shua, I seek your forgiveness, your mercy, and your grace. Receive me into your presence.

signed: ______________________

# 73 Vignettes of

## A. SCRIPTURE

SCRIPTURE is the assemblage of words from the Creator to humanity. When the Saviour referred to Scripture, he was referring to what we have named, The Old Covenant (Testament).

Petros (Peter) includes the scribings of Paulos (Paul) with the 'other Scriptures'.

Paulos (Paul) scribes to Timo Theos (Timothy) that all Scripture is Elohim Spirited and beneficial for doctrine, for proof, for straight cutting, for discipline in justness, to equip the human of Elohim (God) — at shalom.

## B. LIPS, TONGUES & DIALECTS

The word, LANGUAGE, as we know it, does not appear in the manuscripts. At The Tower of Babel, Elohim confounded their LIP. In the Prophets we read of other TONGUES and LIPS.

In Acts, we read that the people spoke in nineteen DIALECTS.

The tongue of the Old Covenant (Testament) from approximately 1500 B.C. to 500 B.C. was Hebraic — with just a few fragments of Aramaic.

Approximately 500 B.C. the scrolls of Dani El (Daniel) and Ezra were scribed in Aramaic.

And from approximately 500 B.C. to 500 A.D., the primary Lip and Tongue was Aramaic— except for the diaspora of the Yah Hudiym (Jews) who migrated from their Holy Land, and spoke Hellene.

NOW HEAR THIS! Aramaic was the lip and tongue of Yah Shua ha Mashiyach (Jesus Christ). We have no record of Yah Shua ha Mashiyach ever having spoken Hellene (Greek).*

*See Webster's Unabridged Dictionary and the Encyclopedia Britannica.

## C. MANUSCRIPTS

A MANUSCRIPT is a manually scribed scribing.

The scribings with which we are concerned, were scribed by scribes, and consist of that which we have named, SCRIPTURE.

## D. SCROLLS

The original Scripture scribed by scribes, were scribed on SCROLLS — elongated sheets of papyrus and/or parchments by holy humans of Elohim (God), as they were moved by the Holy Spirit.

### HEBRAIC AND ARAMAIC OLD COVENANT

Through the years, the Hebraic and Aramaic scrolls were so precisely copied, that if ever there was the slighest error or drip of ink, the entire scroll was discarded. No corrections allowed!

There are still in existence today, accurate copies of the Hebrew Scrolls. The Aramaic Scrolls are difficult to find.

### THE ARAMAIC NEW COVENANT

There exist copies of the New Covenant from the Aramaic known as the Peshita. Being a Semitic Tongue, the Aramaic not only retains the character of the old Covenant, but also clarifies many of the obscure passages of the Hellenic (Greek) text.

exeGeses BIBLES publishes the only Literal Translation & Transliteration of the Aramaic New Covenant in the English language.

## E. FRAGMENTS

The Hellenic Scrolls were not cared for with such diligence. There are more than 5,000 fragments of the New Covenant. However, through the years various linguists have efforted to evaluate the authenticities of the fragments, and we have them in at least two assemblages:

### TEXTUS RECEPTUS

— the Received Text of the New Covenant, is a Hellenic (Bible Greek) text from which most translations are based.

### NOVUM TESTAMENTUM GRAECE

— a more accurate text.*

* SEE: The Name

# 75 Vignettes of

## F. VERSIONS

A **VERSION** is an **ADAPTATION** of a text, usually from one language to another. Hence they are at times erroneously called TRANSLATIONS.

**1. SEPTUAGINT:** If it were not for one very serious error (repeated 6,500 times) the SEPTUAGINT could be called the first LITERAL TRANSLATION of the Old Covenant from the Hebraic and Aramaic to the Hellenic.*

It was prepared by 70 or 72 Scribes in the second and third centuries B.C. for the Yah Hudiym who had left the Holy Land.

*SEE: The Name

**2. MASORETIC TEXT:** Until the eighth century A.D., manuscripts were indicated with what we would call consonants, but no vowels. And until then, sounds were carried on through tradition. The MASORETIC TEXT indicated vowel sounds with 'points' interspersed within the consonants. It is still widely used in Yah Hudaic and Messianic Congregations.

**3. THE AUTHORIZED KING JAMES VERSION of 1611** has stood the test of time for almost four centuries. Still number two on the Best Seller List, it remains number one in the hearts of Scripture lovers. Its acceptance by Bible Lovers is due in part to its beautiful flow of Old English, and to Bible Scholars because it has more research materials than any other version.

**4. THE AMERICAN STANDARD VERSION** was one of the first Versions that transliterated the Name of the Creator in the Old Covenant. It is now out of print.

## G. LITERAL TRANSLATIONS:

A LITERAL TRANSLATION is the precise rendering of a text from one language to another.

**YOUNG'S LITERAL TRANSLATION** is one of the most accurate translations in the English Language. The tenses are most precise, following the Hebraic idioms. The parts of speech are most accurate. In its attempt to follow the Hebrew sentence structure, it is at times difficult to follow the thought line.The name of the Creator is transliterated from the Hebraic and Aramaic of the Old Covenant. However, because the New Covenant was translated from the Hellene, neither the name of the Creator or the Saviour are transliterated.

# Scripture 76

## H. LITERAL TRANSLITERATIONS

### 1. exeGeses parallel BIBLE

**DEFINITIONS**

**exegeses** *plural noun* expositions of Scripture.

**literal** *adjective* precise, exact.

**translation** *noun* the rendering of words from one language to another.

**transliteration** *noun* the rendering of alphabetic letters from one language to another. **Example: Amen** is one of two words that has the same alphabetic letters in every language.

**exeGeses BIBLES** are the only Bibles that translate and transliterate every word of Scripture as precisely as humanly possible (with divine help). And that's why we say,

When you need to know exactly —

— exactly what the Bible says

**exeGeses BIBLES**

the only

**LITERAL**

**TRANSLATIONS & TRANSLITERATIONS**

— ever

There he stood, this giant of a man; and in his majestic voice, he bellowed, "What's the difference between soul and spirit?" And after a dramatic pause, he cozied up to the microphone, placed his elbows on the pulpit, and with a smirk on his face, said, "Frankly, I don't know!" — and 2,500 members of the congregation laughed.

"Make that 2,499," said Herb Jahn, exegete of the Exegeses Bibles and the Aramaic New Covenant. "I sensed his apathy and ignorance were rather pathetic, considering he thought of himself as a theologian.

There was a time Jahn didn't know either, but felt he needed to know in order to be filled with the Spirit. So he researched the two words. His first discovery? **Soul** was mistranslated into more than forty different words — and **spirit** into more than seven.

After he completed that task, he asked his soul, "What would happen if I researched every word of Scripture?" Little did he realize that at age sixty—five, that was the turning point in his life.

Exegete Herb Jahn then invested sixteen years of his life toward one quest — to discover exactly what every word of Scripture means.

In these sixteen years, Jahn has researched every Word of Scripture — more than 14,000 words — word by word — one word at a time.

# 77 Vignettes of

The Proverb of Lemu El:

Who ascended to the heavens
— or descended?

Who gathered the wind in his fists?

Who narrowed the waters in a cloth?

Who raised all the finalities of the earth?

What is his name?

What is the name of his Son
— if you know?

Proverbs 30:4

## WILLFUL MISTRANSLATIONS — — THE NAME OF THE CREATOR:

Would you believe? There is a conspiracy to withhold the Name of the Creator and the name of the Saviour from you.

One Bible Publisher had the exclusive rights to the two finest translations that used the Name of the Creator — and they just let the copyrights expire — Young's Literal Translation, and the American Standard Version.

And then another company took this American Standard Version, substituted the Name of the Creator with the title LORD, and named it The New American Standard Bible.

**1. The Creator declares his name:**

I am the *LORD* **Yah Veh:** that is my name.

**Yesha Yah** *Isaiah* 42:8:

**2. The Creator instructs us to oath by his name:**

Thou shalt *fear* **awe**
*the LORD* **Yah Veh*** thy *God* **Elohim**
and serve him,
and shalt *swear* **oath** by his name.

Deuteronomy 6:13, 10:20

***Yah Veh** means **Eternal Being**

**3. The Creator places one restriction on using his name:**

And ye shall not oath by my name falsely.
Leviticus 19:12

**4.** Although it is veiled in most Versions, the New Covenant, expressly tells us to profess the name of the Creator:

So through him therefore (Yah Shua ha Mashiyach) let us offer the sacrifice of halal to *God* Elohim continually, that is, the fruit of our lips professing his name (Yah Veh).
Hebrews 13:15

## I. WILLFUL MISTRANSLATIONS — THE NAME OF THE SAVIOUR:

**5. The name of the Saviour was pre—ordained:**

And thou shalt call his name *Jesus* **Yah Shua***
for he shall save his people from their sins.

**Matthaios** *Matthew* 1:21

***Yah Shua** means **Eternal Salvation**

**NOTE: Jesus** is an English translation from the Hellenic **Iesous**. As the Hellenes had no **Y**, they substitued it with **Ie**, and suffixed it with the name of the Hellenist deity, **Zeus**.

To further compound the problem, the Saxons changed the Hebraic **V** to a **W** but still pronounced it as **V** — and the **Y** to a **J**, but still pronounced it as **Y**.

**exeGeses BIBLES** are the only Bibles to transliterate every name and title, key it to Strong's Concordance, and define it in the **LEXICON**.

# 79 Vignettes of

## I. WILLFUL MISTRANSLATIONS — THE NAME AND THE TITLE:

**The Authorized King James Version:**

The LORD said unto my Lord, sit thou at my right hand until I make thine enemies thy footstool.

**The exeGeses parallel BIBLE, ready research Version:**

*The LORD said* **An oracle of Yah Veh**
unto my *Lord* **Adonay**,
*sit* **settle** thou at my right *hand*
until I *make* **set** thine enemies
*thy footstool* **the stool of thy feet**.

Psalm 110:1, **Matthaios** *Matthew* 22:44,
**Markos** *Mark* 12:36, **Loukas** *Luke* 20:43,
Acts 2:35, Hebrews 1:13.

Psalm 110:1, as quoted in the New Covenant, is the only verse where an expert may distinguish between LORD (large and small caps), and Lord (upper and lower case) — LORD being a mistranslation of the name, Yah Veh, and Lord, being **Adonay** the title of the Son.

And even in these verses, Strong's Concordance gives both the same spelling, **kurios**, and the same number, {2962}. It is impossible, from the text, to tell which is **Yah Veh**, and which is **Adonay**, or the other words the KJV and other versions translates this word — God, Lord, Master, Sir.

Even being a linguist is of no help here.

# Scripture 80

## AND THEN I ACCIDENTLY (?) DISCOVERED —

There is, however, a slight clue in the **Novum Testamentum Graece** assemblage of New Covenant fragments — and that is this:

Whenever **Adonay** is indicated, it is preceded with article, **the**, or **my**.

Whenever **Yah Veh** is indicated, there is no article preceding. This holds true throughout the New Covenant — except in **Loukas** *Luke*. My Greek teacher was somewhat surprised when I called this to his attention, and suggested I write a paper. Well, this is that paper.

You may verify this from the marginal notes of the Scofield Reference Bible.

**NOTE:** exeGeses BIBLES are the only Bibles that distinguish when [2962] refers to **Yah Veh** or **Adonay**.

## I. WILLFUL MISTRANSLATIONS —
## — THE HOLY SPIRIT

John (Yahn) 3:1—8 tells of the Spirit Birth. Only Young's Literal Translation and exeGeses Bibles translate John 3:8 correctly.

Compare with your version.

The *wind bloweth* **Spirit puffeth**
where *it listeth* **he willeth**,

**NOTE: In the same measure that the Septuagint destroyed the Hebrew and Aramaic character of the Old Covenant , exeGeses Bibles has restored the Hebraic and Aramaic character to the New Covenant.**

When you need to know exactly —
— exactly what the Bible says

**exeGeses BIBLES**

the only

**LITERAL**
**TRANSLATIONS & TRANSLITERATIONS**

— ever

# 81 Vignettes of

## VIGNETTES OF TIME AND SPACE

Name two intangibles that every person has occupied, occupies, and shall occupy from the aeons past, aeons present, and aeons to come.

After reading the heading of this Vignette, may I be so bold as to assume that you said, TIME and SPACE.

TIME and SPACE of aeons past in the foreknowledge of the Creator;
TIME and SPACE of aeons present in this pinpoint we call LIFE;
TIME and SPACE of aeons to come when this 'in body' experience shall have ended, and eternity begun.

How long a TIME is "In the beginning" in the mind of an Eternal Creator?
How long a TIME is "the foreknowledge of Elohim" — when he knew ahead of TIME who would, and who would not receive the atonement his son surrendered for all who would trust in him?
How long a TIME is the patience of Elohim, when the final person to trust in him trusts in him?

Allow me to "fess up" ("confess" to you young whippersnappers). I'm an octogenarian. And when folks ask me how I got to be that old, I say, "As we reckon time, one second at a time."

As humanity reckons time, How old are you? Assuming you are reading this, for every second of your existence, your heart has kept pumping — I'd like to say, "without missing a beat", But then some of have "missed a beat", and we're still here. Ain't God good?

Considering that Elohim has given and is giving and will give you a little more physical TIME on earth, and offers you eternal time with him, what are you doing about it?

See those two squares to the right? Pull out your pen and take a little inventory. Scribe or scribble your responses to the headings.

Let's see if there is any room for improvement.

# Time & Space 82

## MY PAST IN A NUTSHELL

In human measurement, I have occupied ________ years, ____________ days and a few hours, minutes, and seconds.

And here in a nutshell, is what I have accomplished to change the world:

________________________________________

________________________________________

________________________________________

________________________________________

________________________________________

________________________________________

________________________________________

________________________________________

## MY FUTURE IN A NUTSHELL

In human measurement, I would like to occupy ________ years, ____________ days and a few hours, minutes, and seconds more.

And here is what I propose to do to change the world, for as long a TIME as Elohim keeps the plumbing pumping:

________________________________________

________________________________________

________________________________________

________________________________________

________________________________________

________________________________________

________________________________________

________________________________________

# Vignettes of

TIME

To all there is a season
and a time to every desire under the heavens;
a time to birth
and a time to die;
a time to plant
and a time to uproot the planted;
a time to slaughter
and a time to heal;
a time to breach
and a time to build;
a time to weep
and a time to laugh;
a time to chop
and a time to dance;
a time to cast away stones
and a time to gather stones;
a time to embrace
and a time to be far from embracing;
a time to seek
and a time to destroy;
a time to guard
and a time to cast;
a time to rip
and a time to sew;
a time to hush
and a time to word;
a time to love
and a time to hate;
a time of war
and a time of shalom.
What advantage has he who works
in that wherein he toils?
I saw the drudgery
Elohim gave to the sons of humanity
to be humbled therein.
He worked all beautiful in his time;
also he gave eternally in their heart,
so that no human can find out
the work Elohim works
from the top to the end.

Ecclesiastes 3:
from the Companion Translation
of the exeGeses parallel Bible

# Time & Space 84

## THE END OF TIME
### THE OPEN SCROLLETTE

**Apocalypse 10:1—6**

And I see another mighty angel
descend from the heavens
arrayed with a cloud and a rainbow on his head:
and his face as the sun and his feet as pillars of fire:
and in his hand he has an open scrollette:
and he sets his right foot on the sea
and his left on the earth;
and cries with a mega voice exactly as a lion roars:
and when he cries,
seven thunders speak in their own voices.

And when the seven thunders
speak in their own voices,
I am about to scribe:
and I hear a voice from the heavens wording to me,
Seal what the seven thunders spoke
and scribe them not.

And the angel
I see standing on the sea and on the earth
lifts his hand to the heavens,
and oaths in him who lives to the eons of the eons
— who created the heavens and those therein
and the earth and those therein
and the sea and those therein,
that time* is not still:
when measured time as we know it
shall have ended,
and eternity shall have begun.

*Hellene: chronos:

From the Companion Translation
of the exeGeses parallel Bible.

~ ~ ~

Here's an Oldie but Goodie — **SING!**

When the shophar of Yah Veh shall sound
and time shall be no more,
And the morning breaks eternal, bright, and fair,
When the saved of earth shall gather
over on the other shore:
and the roll is called up yonder I'll be there.

On that bright and cloudless morning
when the dead in Mashiyach shall rise,
and the glory of his resurrection share,
when his chosen ones shall gather
to their home beyond the skies:
and the roll is called up yonder I'll be there.

# 85 Vignettes of

**SPACE**

Ever see that marking on your camera that says 'infinity'?

Ever gaze into the skies of the night to see the end of space?

Ever wish you could fly in space and see farther than any human seen?

How is a person like me — like you — able to behold the end of space when space is endless?

SPACE — there sure is a lot of it out there — enough to go around with a little left over.

And Elohim gave you your own little space to be — or not to be. Every TIME you move your finger, Elohim opens up more SPACE — just for you.

Allow me to reminisce. When I was your age (maybe even younger), I was involved in a single's ministry — people without a mate.

One night after a service, we met in a restaurant for fellowship. And this night (it never happened before, or since) I found myself (?) sitting in a booth with three lovely young ladies. Then like a dog with three bones in his mouth, and seeing the reflection in the water, and going after the reflection, and dropping his three bones) I saw another lovely lady across the room. Distance lends enchantment, you know. So I got up to greet (actually, meet) her. When I got back to the booth, lo and behold (whatever that means), a gentlemen sitting in the very spot I sat. And he looked at me with a smirk and said, "Did I take your place?" O I was so clever in those hey days, and I said, "You may sit where I sat, but you'll never take my place."

There it was — another joke at someone else's expence. Most jokes are, you know.

All that to say this: There are a lot of places in those spaces — and Elohim placed you in yours. From the confines of your space, you may muster all the Spirituals — the ministries, the charismata, and the energies, and alter the course of this aeon. And there ain't that many aeons of TIME left ere his parousia takes SPACE.

Ever think about how many anxiously await the parousia of our Adonay, and how few want to go see him tonight.

Be that as it may (another cliche' — rhymes with may) when the Saviour and you and I have our first chat, he'll be wiping all tears from all faces. For what? I'm not too good at guessing, but may I suggest?

# Time & Space 86

1. All the stupid stuff we've done,
2. All the good stuff we've left undone.

May I suggest that he will apocalypse the panorama (unveil the big mural) of LIFE in this TIME and SPACE and show us what we were able to have done — and did not.

Elohim holds us responsible
for what we do
with what we've got.

To whom much is given, much is required — but you knew that.

So what have you got?
And watcha gonna do with it?

**Psalm 8:1—9**

To *the chief Musician* **His Eminence,** upon Gittith,
A Psalm of David.
O *LORD* **Yah Veh**, our *Lord* **Adonay**,
how *excellent* **mighty** is thy name in all the earth!
who hast *set* **given** thy *glory* **majesty** above the heavens.
Out of the mouth of *babes* **infants** and sucklings
hast thou *ordained* **founded** strength
because of *thine enemies* **thy tribulators**,
that thou mightest
*still* **shabbathize** the enemy and the avenger.

When I *consider* **see** thy heavens,
the work of thy fingers,
the moon and the stars,
which thou hast *ordained* **established**;
What is man,
that thou *art mindful of* **rememberest** him?
and the son of *man* **humanity**,
that thou visitest him?
For thou hast made him
a little *lower* **less** than *the angels* **Elohim**,
and hast crowned him
with glory and *honour* **majesty**.
Thou *madest* **hast** him to *have dominion* **reign**
over the works of thy hands;
thou hast put all *things* under his feet:
*All sheep* **Flocks** and oxen,
yea, and the *beasts* **animals** of the field;
The *fowl* **birds** of the *air* **heavens**,
and the fish of the sea,
and whatsoever passeth through the paths of the seas.
O *LORD* **Yah Veh** our *Lord* **Adonay**,
how excellent is thy name in all the earth!

What think ye that he meant, when he said,
"Occupy 'til I come?"

# 87 Vignettes of

## VIGNETTES OF SIGNS

In one of the first labor disputes in my lifetime, I remember the strikers carrying clubs in their hands. And there was an emergency court ruling that the strikers were not allowed to carry clubs, but were allowed to carry signs. So the strikers took baseball bats and tacked a calling card size message — and legally the club became a sign.

Today signs are being used to 'send a message', persuade you to alter your life style, to rile the public — whether justly or unjustly.

- [226] **'oth** *noun* beacon signal, sign
- {4591} **seemion** *verb* signify
- {4592} **seemion** *noun* a sign

Elohim demonstrated the first sign of his new creation in the fourteenth verse of his Book:

**Genesis 1:14, 15**

And Elohim says,
Lights, be in the expanse of the heavens!
— to separate between the day
and between the night;
and for **signs** and for seasons
and for days and years:
and be for lights in the expanse of the heavens
to light up the earth:
— and so be it.

And this very sign that Elohim created for our benefit, the intelligencia has misappropriated in their argument to disprove the existence of the Creator.

This same intelligencia is so proud that they have been able to merely momentarily place a man on the moon — the same moon that Elohim spoke into existence.

Elohim creates, man steps on it. Tell me, which accomplishment is the greater?

## THE SIGN OF QAYIN

The next sign of Elohim was somewhat less complicated — the sign he placed on Qayin:

**Genesis 4:13—15**

And *Cain* **Qayin** said unto *the LORD* **Yah Veh**,
My *punishment* **perversity** is greater than I can bear.
Behold, thou hast *driven* **expelled** me *out* this day
from the face of the *earth* **soil**;
and from thy face shall I be hid;
and I shall be
*a fugitive and a vagabond* **to waver and to wander**
in the earth;
and **so be** it *shall come to pass*,
that every one that findeth me shall *slay* **slaughter** me.
And *the LORD* **Yah Veh** said unto him,
*Therefore* **Thus** whosoever *slayeth Cain* **slaughtereth Qayin**,
*vengeance shall be taken on him*
**he shall be avenged** sevenfold.
And *the LORD* **Yah Veh** set a *mark* **sign** upon *Cain* **Qayin**,
lest any finding him should *kill* **smite** him.

## THE SIGN OF THE RAINBOW

**Genesis 9:12—17**

And *God* **Elohim** said,
This is the *token* **sign** of the covenant
which I *make* **set** between me and **between** you
and every living *creature* **soul** that is with you,
for *perpetual* **eternal** generations:
I *do set* **give** my bow in the cloud,
and it shall be for a *token* **sign** of a covenant
between me and the earth.
And **so be** it *shall come to pass*,
when I *bring* **overcloud** a cloud over the earth,
that the bow shall be seen in the cloud:
And I *will* **shall** remember my covenant,
which is between me and **between** you
and every living *creature* **soul** of all flesh;
and the waters shall *no more* **never again**
become a flood to *destroy* **ruin** all flesh.
And the bow shall be in the cloud;
and I *will look upon* **shall see** it,
that I may remember the *everlasting* **eternal** covenant
between *God* **Elohim**
and **between** every living *creature* **soul** of all flesh
that is upon the earth.
And *God* **Elohim** said unto *Noah* **Noach**,
This is the *token* **sign** of the covenant,
which I have *established* **raised** between me
and all flesh that is upon the earth.

# 89 Vignettes of

## THE SIGN OF THE BIRTH OF THE SAVIOUR

**Loukas 2:8—12**

Therefore *the Lord* **Adonay** himself
shall give you a sign;
Behold, a virgin shall conceive, and *bear* **birth** a son,
and shall call his name *Immanuel* **Immanu El**.
And there were in the same *country* **region**
shepherds abiding in the field,
*keeping watch* **guarding the guard**
over their *flock* **shepherddom** by night.
And, *lo* **behold**, the angel of *the Lord* **Yah Veh**
*came upon* **stood over** them,
and the glory of *the Lord* **Yah Veh**
*shone round about* **haloed** them:
and they *were sore afraid* **awed a mega awe**.
And the angel said unto them,
*Fear* **Awe** not: for, behold,
I *bring you good tidings* **evangelize to you**
of *great joy* **mega cheer**,
which shall be to all people.
For unto you is born this day in the city of David
a Saviour,
which is *Christ the Lord* **ha Mashiyach Adonay**.
And this shall be a sign unto you;
Ye shall find the *babe* **infant**
*wrapped in swaddling clothes* **swathed**,
lying in a manger.

## ENSIGNS

• [5251] **nec** *noun* ensign — the staff, the flag, or both.

### YAH VEH HIMSELF IS OUR ENSIGN

**Exodus 17:15, 16**

And *Moses* **Mosheh** built *an* **a sacrifice** altar,
and called the name of it
*Jehovahnissi* **Yah Veh Nissi**:
For he said,
*Because the LORD hath sworn that*
**The hand of Yah is my ensign:**
*the LORD will have* **Yah Veh shall** war
with *Amalek* **Amaleq**
from generation to generation.

# Signs & Ensigns 90

## THE ENSIGN OF THE SERAPH SERPENTS

**Numbers 21:4—9**

And they *journeyed* **pulled stakes** from mount Hor
by the way of the *Red* **Reed** sea,
to *compass* **surround** the land of Edom:
and the soul of the people
was *much discouraged* **curtailed** because of the way.
And the people *spake* **worded**
against *God* **Elohim**, and against *Moses* **Mosheh**,
Wherefore have ye *brought* **ascended** us *up*
out of *Egypt* **Misrayim** to die in the wilderness?
for there is no bread, neither *is there any* water;
and our soul *loatheth* **abhorreth** this light bread.
And *the LORD* **Yah Veh** sent *fiery* **seraph** serpents
among the people, and they bit the people;
and much people of *Israel* **Yisra El** died.
Therefore the people came to *Moses* **Mosheh**,
and said,
We have sinned,
for we have *spoken* **worded**
against *the LORD* **Yah Veh**, and against thee;
pray unto *the LORD* **Yah Veh**,
that he *take away* **turn aside** the serpents from us.
And *Moses* **Mosheh** prayed for the people.
And *the LORD* **Yah Veh** said unto *Moses* **Mosheh**,
*Make* **Work** thee a *fiery serpent* **seraph**,
and set it upon *a pole* **an ensign**:
and **so be** it *shall come to pass*,
that every one that is bitten,
when he *looketh upon it* **seeth**, shall live.
And *Moses made* **Mosheh worked**
a serpent of *brass* **copper**, and put it upon *a pole* **an ensign**,
and **so be** it *came to pass*,
that if a serpent had bitten any man,
when he *beheld* **looked at**
the serpent of *brass* **copper**,
he lived.

## ETERNAL LIFE

**Yah Chanan 3:14—16**

And **exactly** as *Moses* **Mosheh**
*lifted up* **exalted** the serpent in the wilderness,
even *so* **thus**
must the Son of *man* **humanity** be *lifted up* **exalted**:
That whosoever *believeth* **trusteth** in him
should not *perish* **destruct**, but have eternal life.
For *God so* **Elohim** loved the *world*, **cosmos**
that he gave his only *begotten* **birthed** Son,
that whosoever *believeth* **trusteth** in him
should not *perish* **destruct**
but have *everlasting* **eternal** life.

# 91 Vignettes of

## THE SIGN SEEKING PHARISEES AND SADOQIYM

**Matthaios 16:1—4**

The Pharisees *also* with the *Sadducees* **Sadoqiym** came,
and *tempting* **testing,** *desired* **asked** him
that he *would* **should** shew them
a sign from **the** heavens.
He answered and said unto them,
*When it is* **Being** evening,
ye *say* **word**, *It will be* fair weather:
for the *sky is* **heavens are** *red* **fiery**.
And in the early morning,
*It will be foul weather* **Downpour** to day:
for the *sky is* **heavens are** *red* **fiery** and *lowring* **gloomy**.
*O ye* hypocrites,
ye can **indeed know to**
discern the face of the *sky* **heavens;**
but can ye not *discern*
the signs of the *times* **seasons**?
*A wicked* **An evil** and adulterous generation
seeketh *after* a sign;
and there shall no sign be given unto it,
*but* **except** the sign of the prophet *Jonas* **Yonah**.

**SIGN** is often mistranslated as **wonder**, **miracle**, and even **token**.

Yah Shua performed many signs — turning the water into wine, the ejecting of demons, healing the blind, releasing the tied tongue, healing the lame, and raising the dead — all these, though miraculous, were SIGNS — not to show off his dynamis, but as signs of his deity.

## BEWARE OF IMITATORS!

In the final days there shall be pseudo—apostles, pseudo—prophets, pseudo—ha Mashiyachs. Even Satan shall transform himself into an angel of light.

## PSEUDO APOSTLES

**2 Corinthians 11:13, 14**
For such are *false* **pseudo** apostles,
deceitful workers,
*transforming* **transfiguring** themselves
into the apostles of *Christ* **ha Mashiyach**.
And no marvel; for Satan himself
is *transformed* **transfigured** into an angel of light.
Therefore it is *no great thing* **not mega**
if his ministers also be *transformed* **transfigured**
as the ministers of *righteousness* **justness**;
whose *end* **completion/shalom**
shall be according to their works.

## THE TORAH VIOLATOR

**2 Thessalonians 2:8—11**
And then shall that *Wicked* **torah violator**
be *revealed* **unveiled**,
whom *the Lord* **Adonay** shall consume
with the spirit of his mouth,
and shall *destroy* **inactivate**
with the *brightness* **epiphany**
of his *coming* **parousia**:
*Even him,* whose *coming* **parousia**
is after the *working* **energizing** of Satan
*with* **in** all *power* **dynamis**
and signs and lying *wonders* **omens**,
And *with* **in** all *deceivableness* **delusion**
of *unrighteousness* **injustice**
n them that *perish* **destruct**;
*because* **for** they received not the love of the truth,
*that they might be* **unto their being** saved.

## THE ANTI—HA MASHIYACH

**1 Yah Chanan 2:18 — 22**

Little children, it is the *last time* **final hour**:
and **exactly** as ye have heard
that *antichrist* **the anti—ha Mashiyach** shall come,
even now
are there many *antichrists* **anti—ha Mashiyachs**;
whereby we know that it is the *last time* **final hour**.
They went out from us, but they were not of us;
for if they had been of us,
they *would no doubt* **should** have
*continued* **ever abode** with us:
but *they went out*,
that they might *be made* manifest
that they were not all of us.
But ye have an *unction* **anointing**
from the Holy One,
and ye know all *things*.
I have not *written* **scribed** unto you
because ye know not the truth,
but because ye know it,
and that *no* **not any** lie is of the truth.
Who is a liar *but* **except** he that denieth
that *Jesus* **Yah Shua** is the *Christ* **ha Mashiyach**?
*He is antichrist* **This one is the anti—ha Mashiyach** ,
that denieth the Father and the Son.

**1 Yah Chanan 4:1—3**

Beloved, *believe* **trust** not every spirit,
but *try* **proof** the spirits
whether they are of *God* **Elohim**:
because many *false* **pseudo** prophets
are gone out into the *world* **cosmos**.
*Hereby* **In this** know ye the Spirit of *God* **Elohim**:
Every spirit that *confesseth* **professeth**
that *Jesus Christ* **Yah Shua ha Mashiyach** is come in the flesh
is of *God* **Elohim**:
And every spirit that *confesseth* **professeth** not
that *Jesus Christ* **Yah Shua ha Mashiyach**
is come in the flesh
is not of *God* **Elohim**:
and this is
*that spirit* of *antichrist* **the anti—ha Mashiyach**,
whereof ye have heard that it should come;
and even now already is it in the *world* **cosmos**.

**2 Yah Chanan 7**

*For* **Because** many *deceivers* **seducers**
are entered into the *world* **cosmos**,
who *confess* **profess** not
that *Jesus Christ* **Yah Shua ha Mashiyach** is come in the flesh.
This is *a deceiver* **the seducer**
and *an antichrist* **the anti—ha Mashiyach** .

# 95 Vignettes of

## VIGNETTES OF PRAISE, PSALMS, SONGS, HALALS

Many different words have been mistranslated **praise**. It may well be because the English of the Elizabethan era were not that accustomed to extending hands, clapping, or psalming.

Let us enjoy the full meaning of a few of the words translated **praise**, along with their roots.

- [2158] **zamiyr** *masculine*, **zemirah** *feminine* from
- [2167] a psalm to be accompanied with instrument

But none saith,
Where is *God* **Elohah** my *maker* **worker**,
who giveth *songs* **psalms** in the night;
Iyob 35:10

Thy statutes have been my *songs* **psalms**
in the house of my *pilgrimage* **sojournings**.
Psalm 119:54

- [2167] **zamar** *verb* to psalm: to pluck

*Sing praises* **Psalm** to *the LORD* **Yah Veh**,
which *dwelleth* **settleth** in *Zion* **Siyon**:
*declare* **tell** among the people his *doings* **exploits**.
Psalm 9:11

- {5567} **psallo** *verb* to psalm: to pluck

And that the *Gentiles* **goyim** might
glorify *God* **Elohim** for his mercy;
**exactly** as *it is written* **scribed**,
For this cause
I *will confess* **shall avow** to thee
among the *Gentiles* **goyim**,
and *sing* **psalm** unto thy name.
Romans 15:9, from Psalm 18:49

**So** What *is it then*?
I *will* **shall** pray with the spirit,
and I *will* **shall** pray
with the *understanding* **mind** also:
I *will sing* **shall psalm** with the spirit,
and I *will sing* **shall psalm**
with the *understanding* **mind** also.
1 Corinthians 14:15

Speaking to yourselves in psalms and hymns
and spiritual *songs* **odes**,
singing and *making melody* **psalming** in your heart
to *the Lord* **Adonay**;
Ephesians 5:19

# Praise to Halal 96

• [2172] **zimraw** *noun* a psalm

*Take* **Lift** a psalm,
and *bring hither* **give** the *timbrel* **tambourine**,
the pleasant harp with the *psaltery* **bagpipe**.
*Blow up* **Blast** the *trumpet* **shophar** in the new moon,
in the *time appointed* **full moon**,
on our *solemn feast* **celebration** day.
Psalm 81:2,3

*Sing* **Psalm** unto *the LORD* **Yah Veh** with the harp;
with the harp, and the voice of a psalm.
With trumpets and *sound* **voice** of *cornet* **shophar**
*make a joyful noise* **shout**
*before the LORD* **at the face of Yah Veh**,
the *King* **Sovereign**.
Psalm 98:5,6

• [4210] **mizmor** *noun* a Psalm: used in the title of the Scroll of Psalms.

• {5568} **psalmos** *noun* a psalm

**So** How is it *then*, brethren? when ye come together,
*every one* **each** of you
ath a psalm, hath a doctrine,
hath a tongue, hath *a revelation* **an apocalypse**,
hath *an interpretation* **a translation**.
Let all *things* be *done* unto edifying.
1 Corinthians 14:26

Speaking to yourselves in psalms and hymns
and spiritual *songs* **odes**,
singing and *making melody* **psalming** in your heart
to *the Lord* **Adonay**;
Ephesians 5:19

Let the word of *Christ* **ha Mashiyach**
*dwell in* **indwell** you richly in all wisdom;
*teaching* **doctrinating** and *admonishing* **reminding**
*one another* **yourselves**
in psalms and hymns and spiritual *songs* **odes**,
singing *with grace* **in charism** in your hearts
to *the Lord* **Adonay**.
Colossians 3:16

## EXTENDED HANDS

• [3034] **yadah** *verb* extend hands
This verb is mistranslated, **confess, give thanks, praise**.

**1 Sovereigns 8:33—36**
When thy people *Israel* **Yisra El** be smitten down
*before* **at the face of** the enemy
because they have sinned against thee,
and shall turn again to thee,
and *confess* **extend hands to** thy name, and pray,
and *make supplication* **beseech** unto thee in this house:
Then hear thou in *heaven* **the heavens**,
and forgive the sin of thy people *Israel* **Yisra El**,
and *bring* **return** them *again* unto the *land* **soil**
which thou gavest unto their fathers.
When *heaven is shut up* **the heavens be restrained**,
and there is no rain,
because they have sinned against thee;
if they pray toward this place,
and *confess* **extend hands to** thy name,
and turn from their sin,
when thou *afflictest* **humblest** them:
Then hear thou in *heaven* **the heavens**,
and forgive the sin of thy servants,
and of thy people *Israel* **Yisra El**,
that thou *teach* **direct** them the good way
wherein they should walk,
and give rain upon thy land,
which thou hast given to thy people for an inheritance.

**Psalm 33:1—5**
*Rejoice* **Shout** in *the* L*ORD* **Yah Veh**,
O ye *righteous* **just**:
for *praise is comely for* **halal befitteth** the *upright* **straight**.
*Praise the LORD* **Extend hands to Yah Veh** with harp:
*sing* **psalm** unto him with the *psaltery* **bagpipe**
and *an instrument of ten strings* **decachord**.
Sing unto him a new song;
*play skilfully* **strum well—pleasingly**
with a *loud noise* **blast**.
For the word of *the* L*ORD* **Yah Veh** is *right* **straight**;
and all his works *are done in truth* **trustworthy**.
He loveth *righteousness* **justness** and judgment:
the earth is full
of the *goodness* **mercy**
of *the* L*ORD* **Yah Veh**.

**Psalm 92:1**
A Psalm *or* Song for the *sabbath* **shabbath** day.
It is *a* good *thing*
to *give thanks* **extend hands** unto *the* L*ORD* **Yah Veh**,
and to *sing praises* **psalm** unto thy name,
O *most High* **Elyon**:

# Praise to Halal 98

• [8426] **todah** *noun* extended hand

**Yah Shua 7:19**

And *Joshua* **Yah Shua** said unto Achan,
My son, *give* **set**, I *pray* **beseech** thee,
glory to *the LORD God* **Yah Veh Elohim**
of *Israel* **Yisra El**,
and *make confession* **extend hands** unto him;
and tell me now what thou hast *done* **worked**;
*hide* **conceal** it not from me.

**Yesha Yah 51:3**

For *the LORD* **Yah Veh**
shall *comfort Zion* **sigh over Siyon**:
he *will comfort* **shall sigh over**
all her *waste places* **parched areas**;
and he *will make* **shall set** her wilderness like Eden,
and her *desert* **plain**
like the garden of *the LORD* **Yah Veh**;
*joy* **rejoicing** and *gladness* **cheerfullness**
shall be found therein,
*thanksgiving* **extend hands**,
and the voice of *melody* **psalm**.

**Yirme Yah 17:26**

And they shall come
from the cities of *Judah* **Yah Hudah**,
and *from the places* **round** about *Jerusalem* **Yeru Shalem**,
and from the land of *Benjamin* **Ben Yamin**,
and from the *plain* **lowland**, and from the mountains,
and from the south,
bringing *burnt offerings* **holocausts**, and sacrifices,
and *meat* offerings, and incense,
and *bringing sacrifices of praise* **extending hands**,
unto the house of *the LORD* **Yah Veh**.

# 99 Vignettes of

• [5329] **nazach** *noun* eminent musician used in the titles of several Psalms.
• {103} **aido** *verb* sing

**Ephesians 5:19**
Speaking to yourselves in psalms and hymns
and spiritual *songs* **odes**,
singing and *making melody* **psalming** in your heart
to *the Lord* **Adonay**;

**Colossians 3:16**
Let the word of *Christ* **ha Mashiyach**
*dwell in* **indwell** you richly in all wisdom;
*teaching* **doctrinating** and *admonishing* **reminding**
*one another* **yourselves**
in psalms and hymns and spiritual *songs* **odes**,
singing *with grace* **in charism** in your hearts
to *the Lord* **Adonay**.

**Apocalypse 5:9**
And they sung a new *song* **ode**, *saying* **wording**,
Thou art worthy to take the *book* **scroll**,
and to open the seals thereof:
*for* **because** thou wast *slain* **slaughtered**,
and hast *redeemed* **marketed** us to *God* **Elohim**
by thy blood
out of every *kindred* **scion**, and tongue,
and people, and *nation* **goyim**;

**Apocalypse 14:3**
And they sung as *it were* a new *song* **ode**
*before* **in sight of** the throne,
and *before* **in sight of** the four *beasts* **live beings**,
and the elders:
and no *man* **one** could learn that *song* **ode**
*but* **except** the hundred *and* forty *and* four thousand,
which were *redeemed* **marketed** from the earth.

**Apocalypse 15:3**
And they sing the *song* **ode** of *Moses* **Mosheh**
the servant of *God* **Elohim**,
and the *song* **ode** of the Lamb,
*saying* **wording**,
*Great* **Mega** and marvellous are thy works,
*Lord God Almighty* **Yah Veh El Sabaoth**;
just and true are thy ways,
thou *King* **Sovereign** of *saints* **the holy**.

• [7891] **shiyr** *verb* sing as a stroller

**Psalm 33:1—3**
*Rejoice* **Shout** in *the LORD* **Yah Veh**,
O ye *righteous* **just**:
for *praise is comely for* **halal befitteth** the *upright* **straight**.
*Praise the LORD* **Extend hands to Yah Veh** with harp:
*sing* **psalm** unto him with the *psaltery* **bagpipe**
and *an instrument of ten strings* **decachord**.
Sing unto him a new song;
*play skilfully* **strum well—pleasingly**
with a *loud noise* **blast**.

# Praise to Halal 100

**Psalm 105:1—3**

O *give thanks* **extend hands** unto *the LORD* **Yah Veh**;
call upon his name:
make known his *deeds* **exploits** among the people.
Sing unto him, *sing psalms* **psalm** unto him:
*talk* **meditate** ye of all his *wondrous works* **marvels**.
*Glory* **Halal** ye in his holy name:
let the heart of them *rejoice* **cheer**
that seek *the LORD* **Yah Veh**.

• [7892] **shiyr** *noun* a song

**Yesha Yah 5:1**

*Now* **I beseech**,
*will* **shall** I sing to my *wellbeloved* **beloved**
a song of my beloved touching his vineyard.
My *wellbeloved* **beloved** hath a vineyard
in *a very fruitful hill* **the horn of the son of oil:**

• {5214} **humneo** *verb* to hymn

**Matthaios 26:30, Markos 14:26**

And when they had *sung an hymn* **hymned**,
they went out into the mount of Olives.

**Acts 16:25**

And at midnight,
Paulos and Silas pray and hymn to Elohim:
and the prisoners hear them.

**Hebrews 2:12: from Psalm 22:22**

*Saying* **Wording**,
I *will declare* **shall evangelize** thy name
unto my brethren,
in the midst of the *church* **ecclesia**
*will I sing praise* **shall I hymn** unto thee.

• [7440] **rinnah** *noun* a shout

**Psalm 30:4, 5**

*Sing* **Psalm** unto *the LORD* **Yah Veh**,
O ye *saints* **mercied** of his,
and *give thanks* **extend hands**
at the *remembrance* **memorial** of his holiness.
For his *anger endureth* **wrath is** but a *moment* **blink**;
in his *favour* **pleasure** is life:
weeping may *endure* **stay** for *a night* **an evening**,
but *joy cometh* **shouting** in the morning.

**Psalm 42:4**

When I remember these *things*,
I pour out my soul in me:
for I had *gone* **passed on** with the multitude,
I *went* **walked gently** with them to the house of *God* **Elohim**,
with the voice of *joy* **shouting**
and *praise* **extend hands**,
with a multitude that *kept holyday* **celebrated**.

**Psalm 47:1**

O clap your *hands* **palms**, all ye people;
shout unto *God* **Elohim** with the voice of *triumph* **shouting**.

# 101 Vignettes of

• [7442] **ranan** *verb* to shout

**Iyob 38:1—13**

Then *the LORD* **Yah Veh**
answered *Job* **Iyob** out of the *whirlwind* **storm**, and said,
Who is this that darkeneth counsel
by *words* **utterances** without knowledge?
Gird up *now* **I beseech,** thy loins like a *man* **mighty**;
for I *will demand* **shall ask** of thee,
and *answer thou me* **let me know**.
Where wast thou
when I *laid the foundations of* **founded** the earth?
*declare* **tell**,
if thou *hast understanding* **knowest discernment**.
Who *hath laid* **set** the *measures* **measurements** *thereof*,
if thou knowest?
or who hath stretched the line upon it?
Whereupon are the foundations *thereof fastened* **sunk**?
or who *laid* **poured** the corner stone *thereof*;
When the morning stars *sang* **shouted** together,
and all the sons of *God* **Elohim** shouted *for joy*?
Or who *shut up* **hedged in** the sea with doors,
when it *brake forth* **gushed**,
*as if it had* **when it** issued out of the womb?
When I *made* **set** the cloud
*the garment thereof* **for a robe**,
and *thick* **dripping** darkness
*a swaddling band for it* **for a swathe**,
And brake up for it my *decreed place* **statute**,
and set bars and doors,
And said, Hitherto shalt thou come,
but *no further* **add not**:
and here shall *thy proud* **the pomp of thy** wav *be stayed* **set**?
Hast thou *commanded* **misvahed** the morning
since thy days;
and caused the *dayspring* **dawn** to know his place;
That it might take hold of the *ends* **wings** of the earth,
that the wicked might be shaken out of it?

**Yesha Yah 12:6**

*Cry out* **Resound** and shout,
thou *inhabitant* **settlers** of *Zion* **Siyon**:
for great is the Holy One of *Israel* **Yisra El**
in the midst of thee.

**Yesha Yah 44:23**

*Sing* **Shout**, O ye heavens;
for *the LORD* **Yah Veh** hath *done* **worked** it:
shout, ye *lower parts of the* **nethermost** earth:
break forth into *singing* **shouting**, ye mountains,
O forest, and every tree therein:
for *the LORD* **Yah Veh** hath redeemed *Jacob* **Yaaqov**,
and *glorified* **adorned** himself in *Israel* **Yisra El**.

• [7445] **renanah** *noun* a shout

**Psalm 63:5**

My soul shall be satisfied
as *with* marrow and *fatness* **fat**;
and my mouth shall *praise* **halal** *thee*
with *joyful* **shouting** lips:

# Praise to Halal 102

**Psalm 100:1,2**
A Psalm of *praise* **extended hands**.
*Make a joyful noise* **Shout** unto *the LORD* **Yah Veh**,
all ye *lands* **earth**.
Serve *the LORD* **Yah Veh** with *gladness* **cheerfullness**:
come *before* **at** his *presence* **face** with *singing* **shouting**.
~ ~ ~
• [7623] [7624] **shabach** *verb* adore, adulate, halal

**Psalm 63:3**
Because thy *loving kindness* **mercy** is better than life,
my lips shall *praise* **laud** thee.

**Psalm 106:47**
Save us, O *LORD* **Yah Veh** our *God* **Elohim**,
and gather us from among the *heathen* **goyim**,
to *give thanks* **extend hands** unto thy holy name,
and to *triumph* **laud** in thy *praise* **halal**.

**Psalm 145:4**
*One generation* **Generation to generation**
shall *praise* **laud** thy works *to another*,
and shall *declare* **tell** thy *mighty acts* **might**.

**Dani El 2:23**
I thank thee, and *praise* **laud** thee,
O thou *God* **Elah** of my fathers,
who hast given me wisdom and might,
and hast made known unto me now
what we *desired* **requested** of thee:
for thou hast *now* made known unto us
the *king's matter* **sovereign's utterance**.

• {1867} **epaineo** *verb* laud, applaud

**Loukas 16:8**
And *the Lord* **Adonay**
*commended* **halaled** the unjust *steward* **administrator**,
because he had done *wisely* **thoughtfully**:
for the *children* **sons** of this *world* **eon** are
in their generation
*wiser* **more thoughtful** than the *children* **sons** of light.

# 103 Vignettes of

**Romans 15:11**
And again,
*Praise the Lord* **Halalu Yah**, all ye *Gentiles* **goyim**;
and *laud* **halal** him, all ye people.
And again, *Esaias saith* **Yesha Yah wordeth**,
There shall be a root of *Jesse* **Yishay**,
and he that shall rise
to *reign* **rule** over the *Gentiles* **goyim**;
in him shall the *Gentiles trust* **goyim hope**.

**1 Corinthians 11:22**
*What?* **Indeed!**
have ye not houses to eat and to drink in?
or *despise* **disesteem** ye
the *church* **ecclesia** of *God* **Elohim**,
and shame them that have not?
What shall I say to you? shall I *praise* **halal** you in this?
I *praise* **halal** *you* not.

- {136} **ainos** *noun* from {1868} halal
- {1868} **epainos** *noun* **laud, applause, halal**

**Matthaios 21:16**
And said unto him, Hearest thou what these *say* **word**?
And *Jesus saith* **Yah Shua wordeth** unto them, Yea;
have ye never ever read,
out of the mouth of babes and *sucklings* **nipplers**
thou hast *perfected praise* **prepared halal**?

**Ephesians 1:11—14**
In whom also
we have *obtained an inheritance* **inherited**,
being *predestinated* **predetermined**
according to the *purpose* **prothesis**
of him who *worketh* **energizeth** all *things*
after the counsel of his own will:
*That we should be* **Unto our being**
to the *praise* **halal** of his glory,
who *first trusted* **forehoped** in *Christ* **ha Mashiyach**.
In whom ye also *trusted*,
after that ye heard the word of truth,
the *gospel* **evangelism** of your salvation:
in whom also, *after that ye believed* **having trusted**,
ye were sealed
with that holy Spirit of *promise* **pre—evangelism**,
Which is the *earnest* **pledge** of our inheritance
*until* **unto** the redemption
of the *purchased possession* **acquisition**,
unto the *praise* **halal** of his glory.

# Praise to Halal 104

**THE LIVING HOPE**

**1 Petros 1:3—7**

*Blessed* **Eulogized** be the *God* **Elohim** and Father
of our *Lord Jesus Christ* **Adonay Yah Shua ha Mashiyach**,
which according to his *abundant* **vast** mercy
hath *begotten* **rebirthed** us *again* unto a *lively* **living** hope
by the resurrection of *Jesus Christ* **Yah Shua ha Mashiyach**
from the dead,
To an inheritance
incorruptible, and *undefiled* **unpolluted**,
*and that fadeth not away* — **amaranthine**,
*reserved in heaven for* **guarded in the heavens unto** you,
Who are *kept* **garrisoned**
*by* **in** the *power* **dynamis** of *God* **Elohim**
through *faith* **trust** unto salvation
*ready* **prepared** to be *revealed* **unveiled**
in the *last time* **final season**.
Wherein ye *greatly rejoice* **jump for joy**,
though now for a *season* **little**, if need be,
ye are *in heaviness* **sorrowed**
*through manifold temptations* **in divers testings**:
That the *trial* **proofing** of your *faith* **trust**,
being much more precious
than of gold that *perisheth* **destructeth**,
though it be *tried with* **proofed through** fire,
might be found unto *praise* **halal** and honour and glory
at the *appearing* **apocalypse**
of *Jesus Christ* **Yah Shua ha Mashiyach**:

• [8416] **tehillah** *noun* from [1984] a hymn of halal

**Psalm 22:3**

But thou art holy,
O thou that *inhabitest* **settlest**
**in** the *praises* **halals** of *Israel* **Yisra El**.

**Psalm 22:22—25**

I *will declare* **shall scribe** thy name unto my brethren:
in the midst of the congregation
*will I praise* **shall I halal** thee.
Ye that *fear the LORD* **awe Yah Veh**, *praise* **halal** him;
all ye the seed of *Jacob* **Yaaqov**, *glorify* **honour** him;
and *fear* **dodge** him, all ye the seed of *Israel* **Yisra El**.
For he hath not despised nor *abhorred* **abominated**
the *affliction* **humbling** of the *afflicted* **humble**;
neither hath he hid his face from him;
but when he cried unto him, he heard.
My *praise* **halal** shall be of thee
in the great congregation:
I *will pay* **shall shalam** my vows
*before* **in front of** them that *fear* **awe** him.

# 105 Vignettes of

• [1984] **halal** *verb* the highest expression of reverence: the root of Hallalu Yah.

**Ezra 3:10,11**

And when the builders laid the foundation
of the *temple* **manse** of *the LORD* **Yah Veh**,
they *set* **stood** the priests
*in their apparel* **enrobed** with trumpets,
and the *Levites* **Leviym** the sons of Asaph with cymbals,
to *praise the LORD* **halal Yah Veh**,
after the *ordinance* **hand**
of David *king* **sovereign** of *Israel* **Yisra El**.
And they *sang* **answered** together by course
in *praising* **halaling**
and *giving thanks* **extending hands**
unto *the LORD* **Yah Veh**;
because he is good,
for his mercy *endureth for ever* **is eternal**
toward *Israel* **Yisra El**.
And all the people shouted with a great *shout* **shouting**,
when they *praised the LORD* **halaled Yah Veh**,
because the foundation
of the house of *the LORD* **Yah Veh** was laid.

**Psalm 150:1—6**

*Praise ye the LORD* **Halalu Yah**.
*Praise God* **Halal El** in his *sanctuary* **holies**:
*praise* **halal** him
in the *firmament* **expanse** of his *power* **strength**.
*Praise* **Halal** him
for his *mighty acts* **might**:
*praise* **Halal** him
according to his *excellent* **abundant** greatness.
*Praise* **Halal** him
with the *sound* **blast** of the *trumpet* **shophars**:
*praise* **halal** him
with the *psaltery* **bagpipe** and harp.
*Praise* **Halal** him
with the *timbrel* **tambourine** and **round** dance:
*praise* **halal** him
with *stringed instruments* **strummers**
and *organs* **woodwinds**.
*Praise* **Halal** him
upon the *loud* **hearkening** cymbals:
*praise* **halal** him
upon the *high sounding* **clanging** cymbals.
Let *every thing that hath breath* **all that breatheth**
*praise the LORD* **halal Yah**.
*Praise ye the LORD* **Hallalu Yah**.

# Praise to Halal 106

• {239} **allelouia** *verb* combination of [1984 ]**halal** and• [3050] **Yah**

**Apocalypse 19:1—6**

And after these *things* I heard a *great* **mega** voice
of *much people* **many multitudes** in *heaven* **the heavens**,
*saying* **wording**, *Alleluia* **Halalu Yah**;
Salvation, and glory, and honour, and *power* **dynamis**,
unto *the Lord* **Yah Veh** our *God* **Elohim**:
*For* **Because** true and *righteous* **just** are his judgments:
*for* **because** he hath judged the *great* **mega** whore,
which *did corrupt* **corrupted** the earth
*with* **in** her *fornication* **whoredom**,
and hath avenged the blood of his servants
*at* **from** her hand.
And *again* **secondly** they said, *Alleluia* **Halalu Yah**.
And her smoke *rose up* **ascended**
*for ever and ever* **unto the eons of the eons**.

And the four and twenty elders
and the four *beasts* **live beings** fell *down*
and worshipped *God* **Elohim** that sat on the throne,
*saying* **wording**, Amen; *Alleluia* **Halalu Yah**.
And a voice came out of the throne, *saying* **wording**,
*Praise* **Halal** our *God* **Elohim**, all ye his servants,
and ye that *fear* **awe** him,
both *small* **minute** and *great* **mega**.
And I heard
as *it were* the voice of a *great* **vast** multitude,
and as the voice of many waters,
and as the voice of mighty thunderings,
*saying* **wording**, *Alleluia* **Halalu Yah**:
*for* **because**
*the Lord God omnipotent* **Yah Veh El Sabaoth** reigneth.

# 107 Vignettes of

## SEASONS

Contrary to public opinion, Yah Veh did not plan our lives to be a pile of dos and don'ts — rather to be season after season of feasting, fasting, celebration, relaxation, and worship.

## PREAMBLE

**Leviticus 23:1—5**

And *the LORD spake* **Yah Veh worded**
unto *Moses* **Mosheh**, saying,
*Speak* **Word** unto the *children* **sons** of *Israel* **Yisra El**,
and say unto them,
*Concerning* the *feasts* **seasons** of *the LORD* **Yah Veh**,
which ye shall *proclaim* **recall** to be holy convocations,
even these are my *feasts* **seasons**.

Six days shall work be *done* **worked**:
but the seventh day
is the *sabbath* **shabbath** of *rest* **shabbathism**,
an holy convocation;
ye shall *do* **work** no work *therein*:
it is the *sabbath* **shabbath** of *the LORD* **Yah Veh**
in all your *dwellings* **settlements**.

## SEASONS TO RECALL

These are the *feasts* **seasons** of *the LORD* **Yah Veh**,
even holy convocations,
which ye shall *proclaim* **recall** in their seasons.

• [4150] **mowed** *noun* (mo—ade′) appointment. In Scripture, refers to appointed seasons, and appointed congregations.

• [7121] **qara′** *verb* call out, recall.
• [4744] **miqra′** *noun* a calling out of a person or place.

## SEASON OF PASACH

*In the fourteenth day of the first month*
**In the first month, on the fourteenth of the month,**
*at even* **between evenings**
is *the LORD'S passover* **Yah Veh's pasach**.

**pasach** *transliterated noun* [6453] **pecach** {3957} **pasach.** A celebration of Elohim's protection; a celebration sacrifice of a lamb; Adonay Yah Shua ha Mashiyach as our protection; often mistranslated passover.

## YAH SHUA GUARDED THE PASACH
## THE FINAL PASACH OF YAH SHUA

**Matthaios 26:17:30**

Now the first day
of the *feast of unleavened bread* **mazzah**
the disciples came to *Jesus* **Yah Shua**,
*saying* **wording** unto him,
Where *wilt* **willest** thou that we prepare for thee
to eat the *passover* **pasach**?
And he said, Go into the city to *such a man* **so and so**,
and say unto him, The *Master saith* **Doctor wordeth**,
My *time* **season** is *at hand* **nigh**;
I *will keep* **shall do** the *passover* **pasach** at thy house
with my disciples.
And the disciples did
as *Jesus* **Yah Shua** had *appointed* **ordered** them;
and they *made ready* **prepared** the *passover* **pasach**.
Now when *the even was come* **being evening**,
he *sat down* **reposed** with the twelve.
And as they did eat, he said,
*Verily I say* **Amen! I word** unto you,
that one of you shall betray me.
And they were *exceeding* **extremely** sorrowful,
and began *every one* **each** of them to *say* **word** unto him,
*Lord* **Adonay**, is it I?
And he answered and said,
He that *dippeth* **baptizeth** his hand with me in the dish,
the same shall betray me.
The Son of *man* **humanity indeed** goeth
**exactly** as it is *written of* **scribed concerning** him:
but woe unto that *man* **human**
*by* **through** whom the Son of *man* **humanity** is betrayed!
it had been good for that *man* **human**
if he had not been *born* **birthed**.
*Then Judas* **But Yah Hudah**, which betrayed him,
answered and said, *Master* **Rabbi**, is it I?
He *said* **worded** unto him, Thou hast said.

## THE FINAL EUCHARIST
## OF YAH SHUA

And as they were eating, *Jesus* **Yah Shua** took bread,
and *blessed* it **eulogized** and brake it,
and gave it to the disciples, and said,
Take, eat; this is my body.
And he took the cup, and *gave thanks* **eucharistized**,
and gave it to them, *saying* **wording**, Drink ye all of it;
For this is my blood of the new *testament* **covenant**,
which is *shed* **poured** for many
*for* **unto** the *remission* **forgiveness** of sins.
But I *say* **word** unto you,
I *will* **shall** *not* **never no way** drink henceforth
of this *fruit* **produce** of the vine,
until that day when I drink it new with you
in my Father's *kingdom* **sovereigndom**.
And when they had *sung an hymn* **hymned**,
they went out into the mount of Olives.

# 109 Vignettes of

## SEASON OF MAZZAH

• [4682 mazzah] {106 azumos} **mazzah**
*transliterated noun* unfermented bakery.

**Leviticus 23:6—14**
And on the fifteenth day of the same month
is the *feast* **celebration** of *unleavened bread* **mazzah**
unto *the LORD* **Yah Veh**:
seven days ye *must* **shall** eat *unleavened bread* **mazzah**.
In the first day ye shall have an holy convocation:
ye shall *do* **work** no *servile* **service** work therein.
But ye shall *offer an offering made by fire* **oblate a firing**
unto *the LORD* **Yah Veh** seven days:
in the seventh day is an holy convocation:
ye shall *do* **work** no *servile* **service** work *therein*.

**Exodus 12:15—20**
Seven days shall ye eat *unleavened bread* **mazzah**;
*even* **surely** the first day
ye shall *put away leaven* **shabbathize yeast**
out of your houses:
for whosoever eateth *leavened bread* **fermentation**
from the first day until the seventh day,
that soul shall be cut off from *Israel* **Yisra El**.

And in the first day there shall be an holy convocation,
and in the seventh day
there shall be an holy convocation to you;
no *manner of* work shall be *done* in them,
*save* **except** that which every *man* **soul** must eat,
that only may be *done* **worked** of you.
And ye shall *observe* **guard**
the *feast of unleavened bread* **mazzah**;
for in this selfsame day have I brought your *armies* **hosts**
out of the land of *Egypt* **Misrayim**:
therefore shall ye *observe* **guard** this day
in your generations
by an *ordinance for ever* **eternal statute**.
In the first *month*,
on the fourteenth day of the month at even,
ye shall eat *unleavened bread* **mazzah**,
until the one and twentieth day of the month at even.
Seven days
shall there be no *leaven* **yeast** found in your houses:
for whosoever eateth that which is *leavened* **fermented**,
even that soul shall be cut off
from the *congregation* **witness** of *Israel* **Yisra El**,
whether he be a *stranger* **sojourner**,
or *born* **native** in the land.

## SEASON OF HARVEST FIRSTS

**Leviticus 23:9—14**

And *the LORD spake* **Yah Veh**
**worded** unto *Moses* **Mosheh**, saying,
*Speak* **Word** unto the *children* **sons** of *Israel* **Yisra El**,
and say unto them,
When ye be come into the land which I give unto you,
and shall *reap* **harvest** the harvest thereof,
then ye shall bring *a sheaf* **an omer**
of the *firstfruits* **firsts** of your harvest unto the priest:
And he shall wave the *sheaf* **omer**
*before the LORD* **at the face of Yah Veh**,
*to be accepted for you* **at your pleasure**:
on the morrow after the *sabbath* **shabbath**
the priest shall wave it.
And ye shall *offer* **work** that day
when ye wave the *sheaf* **omer**
an he lamb *without blemish* **integrious**
*of the first year* — **a yearling son**
for a *burnt offering* **holocaust** unto *the LORD* **Yah Veh**.

Ye shall eat *nothing leavened* **naught fermented**;
in all your *habitations* **settlements**
shall ye eat *unleavened bread* **mazzah**.
And the *meat* offering thereof
shall be two *tenth deals of fine* **tenths** flour
*mingled* **mixed** with oil,
*an offering made by fire* **a firing** unto *the LORD* **Yah Veh**
for a *sweet savour* **scent of rest**:
and the *drink offering* **libation** thereof shall be of wine,
the fourth *part* of an hin.
And ye shall eat neither bread, nor parched *corn*,
nor *green ears* **of the orchard**,
until *the selfsame* **that** day that ye have brought
an *offering* **qorban** unto your *God* **Elohim**:
it shall be *a* **an eternal** statute *for ever*
throughout your generations
in all your *dwellings* **settlements**.

# 111 Vignettes of

## SEASON OF PENTECOST IN THE OLD COVENANT

• {4005} **pentekoste** *noun* fiftieth

Although the word **pentecost** is derived from the Hellene, we have applied the word to the Old Covenant seasons of **fiftieths**.

**PENTECOST** — fiftieth follows the seven sevens - a Season of Celebration of Harvest.

**Leviticus 23:15—22**

And ye shall *count* **scribe** unto you
from the morrow after the *sabbath* **shabbath**,
from the day
that ye brought the *sheaf* **omer** of the wave *offering*;
seven *sabbaths* **shabbaths** shall be *complete* **integrious**:
Even unto the morrow
after the seventh *sabbath* **shabbath**
shall ye *number* **scribe** fifty days;
and ye shall *offer* **oblate** a new *meat* offering
unto *the LORD* **Yah Veh**.
Ye shall bring out of your *habitations* **settlements**
two wave *loaves* **breads** of two *tenth deals* **tenths**;
they shall be of *fine* flour;
they shall be baken with *leaven* **fermentation**;
they are the firstfruits unto *the LORD* **Yah Veh**.

And ye shall *offer* **oblate** with the bread
seven lambs *without blemish* **integrious**
*of the first year* — **yearling sons**,
and one *young* bullock **son of the oxen**, and two rams:
they shall be for a *burnt offering* **holocaust**
unto *the LORD* **Yah Veh**,
with their *meat* offering, and their *drink offerings* **libations**,
*even an offering made by fire* **a firing**,
*of sweet savour* **a scent of rest** unto *the LORD* **Yah Veh**.
Then ye shall *sacrifice* **work** one *kid* **buck** of the goats
for *a sin offering* **the sin**,
and two lambs *of the first year* **yearling sons**
for a sacrifice of *peace offerings* **shelamim**.
And the priest shall wave them
with the bread of the firstfruits for a wave *offering*
*before the LORD* **at the face of Yah Veh**,
with the two lambs:

they shall be holy to *the LORD* **Yah Veh** for the priest.
And ye shall proclaim on the selfsame day,
that it may be an holy convocation unto you:
ye shall *do* **work** no *servile* **service** work *therein*:
it shall be *a* **an eternal** statute *for ever*
in all your *dwellings* **settlements**
throughout your generations.
And when ye *reap* **harvest** the harvest of your land,
thou shalt not *make clean riddance of* **finish off**
the *corners* **edges** of thy field
when thou *reapest* **harvestest**,
neither shalt thou *gather* **glean**
any gleaning of thy harvest:
thou shalt leave them unto the *poor* **humbled**,
and to the *stranger* **sojourner**:
*I am the LORD* **I — Yah Veh** your *God* **Elohim**.

## THE SEASON OF PENTECOST IN THE NEW COVENANT

It has been said that Pentecost in the Old Covenant is the birthday of Yah Hudaism; and the Pentecost in the New Covenant is the birthday of the Ecclesia.

**1 Corinthians 15:20**

But now is *Christ* **ha Mashiyach** risen from the dead,
and become the *firstfruits* **firstlings** of them that slept.

**Acts 2:2—47**

And *when* **in** the day of Pentecost
*was fully come* **being fulfilled/shalamed**,
they were all *with one accord* **in unanimity** in one place.
And **so be it,** suddenly
*there came a sound* — **an echo** from the heavens
as of a *rushing mighty wind* **bearing forceful puff**,
and it filled **full** all the house where they were sitting.
And there appeared unto them
*cloven* **divided** tongues like as of fire,
and it sat upon each *one* of them.
And they were all filled **full** with the Holy *Ghost* **Spirit**,
and began to speak with other tongues,
**exactly** as the Spirit gave them utterance.
And there were
*dwelling* **settling** at *Jerusalem* **Yeru Shalem**
*Jews* **Yah Hudiym**, *devout* **well—received** men,
out of every *nation* **goyim** under heavens.

Parthians, and *Medes* **Maday**, and *Elamites* **Elamiym**,
and *the dwellers* **they who settled** in Mesopotamia,
and in *Judaea* **Yah Hudah**, and Cappadocia,
in Pontus, and Asia,
Phrygia, and Pamphylia, in *Egypt* **Misrayim**,
and in the parts of Libya about Cyrene,
and *strangers of Rome* **the Romans residing there**,
*Jews* **Yah Hudiym** and proselytes,
Cretes and *Arabians* **Arabs**,
we do hear them speak in our tongues
the *wonderful works* **magnificence** of *God* **Elohim**.
And they were all *amazed* **astounded**,
and were *in doubt* **thoroughly perplexed**,
*saying* **wording** one to another,
What *meaneth* **willeth** this **to be**?
Others *mocking said* **jeering worded**,
These men are full of new sweet wine.

## THE FIRST MESSAGE OF PETROS

But *Peter* **Petros**, standing *up* with the eleven,
lifted *up* his voice, and *said* **uttered** unto them,
*Ye men of Judaea* **Men — Yah Hudiym**,
and all ye that *dwell* **settle** at *Jerusalem* **Yeru Shalem**,
be this known unto you,
and hearken to my *words* **rhema**:

## The PROPHECY OF YAH EL FULFILLED/SHALAMED

For these are not *drunken* **intoxicated**,
as ye *suppose* **perceive**,
*seeing* **indeed** it is but the third hour of the day.
But this is that which was *spoken* **said**
*by* **through** the prophet *Joel* **Yah El**;
And it shall *come to pass* **become** in the *last* **final** days,
*saith God* **wordeth Elohim**,
I *will* **shall** pour *out* of my Spirit upon all flesh:
and your sons and your daughters shall prophesy,
and your *young men* **youths** shall see visions,
and your *old men* **elders** shall dream dreams:
And **yet indeed**
on my servants and on my *hand maidens* **maids**
I *will* **shall** pour *out* in those days of my Spirit;
and they shall prophesy:
And I *will shew* **shall give**
*wonders* **omens** in **the** *heaven* **the heavens** above,
and signs in the earth *beneath* **below**;
blood, and fire, and vapour of smoke:
The sun shall be turned into darkness,
and the moon into blood,
*before* **ere** the *great* **mega** and *notable* **epiphanous**
day of *the Lord* **Yah Veh** come:
And **so be** it *shall come to pass*,
that **everyone** — whosoever
shall call on the name of *the Lord* **Yah Veh**
shall be saved.

## YAH SHUA IS ADONAY AND HA MASHIYACH

*Ye men of Israel* **Men — Yisra Eliym**, hear these words;
*Jesus of Nazareth* **Yah Shua the Nazarene**,
a man *approved* of *God* **Elohim, shown** among you
by *miracles* **dynamis** and *wonders* **omens** and signs,
which *God* **Elohim** did *by* **through** him
in the midst of you,
**exactly** as ye yourselves also know:
Him, being *delivered* **given over**
by the *determinate* **decreed** counsel
and *foreknowledge* **prognosis** of *God* **Elohim**,
ye have taken,
and *by wicked* **through untorahed** hands
have *crucified* **staked** and *slain* **taken out**:
Whom *God* **Elohim** hath raised *up*,
having loosed the *pains* **travail** of death:
*because* **as** it was not possible
that he should be *holden of* **overpowered by** it.

# 115 Vignettes of

## THE PROPHECY OF DAVID FULFILLED/SHALAMED

For David *speaketh concerning* **wordeth unto** him,
I foresaw *the Lord always* **Yah Veh through all time**
*before* **in sight of** my face,
for he is *on* **at** my right *hand*,
that I should not be *moved* **shaken**:
*Therefore* **Because of this** did my heart rejoice,
and my tongue *was glad* **jumped for joy**;
*moreover* **yet** also my flesh shall *rest* **nest** in hope:
Because thou
*wilt* **shalt** not leave my soul in *hell* **sheol/hades**,
neither *wilt* **shalt** thou
*suffer thine Holy One* **give thy Merciful**
to see corruption.
Thou hast made known to me the ways of life;
thou shalt *make me full of joy* **shalam me with rejoicing**
with thy *countenance* **face**.
Men and brethren,
*let* **allow** me *freely speak* **to boldly say** unto you
*of* **concerning** the patriarch David,
that he is both dead and *buried* **entombed**,
and his *sepulchre* **tomb** is with us unto this day.
*Therefore* **So** being a prophet,
and knowing that *God* **Elohim**
had *sworn with* **oathed** an oath to him,
that of the fruit of his loins, according to the flesh,
he *would* **should** raise *up Christ* **ha Mashiyach**
to sit on his throne;
He *seeing* **foreseeing** this *before*
spake of the resurrection of *Christ* **ha Mashiyach**,
that his soul was not left in *hell* **sheol/hades**,
neither his flesh did see corruption.
This *Jesus* **Yah Shua** hath *God* **Elohim** raised *up*,
whereof we all are witnesses.
*Therefore* **So**
being *by* **at** the right *hand* of *God* **Elohim** exalted,
and having *received* **taken** of the Father
the *promise* **pre—evangelism** of the Holy *Ghost* **Spirit**,
he hath *shed forth* **poured** this,
which ye now see and hear.
For David is not ascended into the heavens:
but he *saith* himself **wordeth**,
*the LORD said* **An oracle of Yah Veh**
unto my *Lord* **Adonay**,
Sit thou *on* **at** my right *hand*,
Until I *make* **place** thy *foes* **enemies**
*thy footstool* **the stool of they feet**.
*Therefore* **So** let all the house of *Israel* **Yisra El**
know *assuredly* **certainly**,
that *God* **Elohim** hath made the same *Jesus* **Yah Shua**,
whom ye have *crucified* **staked**,
both *Lord* **Adonay** and *Christ* **ha Mashiyach**.

## TAKING THE GRATUITY OF THE HOLY SPIRIT

Now when they heard this,
they were *pricked* **pierced** in their heart,
and said unto *Peter* **Petros** and to the rest of the apostles,
Men and brethren, what shall we do?
For the *promise* **pre—evangelism** is unto you,
and to your children, and to all that are afar off,
even as many
as *the Lord* **Yah Veh** our *God* **Elohim** shall call.
And with many other words
did he *testify* **witness** and *exhort* **beseech**,
*saying* **wording**,
*Save yourselves* **Be ye saved**
from this *untoward* **crooked** generation.

## THE FIRST ECCLESIA

*Then* **So indeed**
they that *gladly* **with pleasure** received his word
were baptized:
and *the same* **that** day there were added *unto them*
about three thousand souls.
And they continued stedfastly
in the apostles' doctrine and *fellowship* **communion**,
and in breaking of bread, and in prayers.

And *fear came* **awe became** upon every soul:
and many *wonders* **omens** and signs
*were done by* **became through** the apostles.
Then *Peter* **Petros** said unto them,
Repent, and be baptized *every one* **each** of you
in the name of *Jesus Christ* **Yah Shua ha Mashiyach**
*for* **unto** the *remission* **forgiveness** of sins,
and ye shall *receive* **take**
the *gift* **gratuity** of the Holy *Ghost* **Spirit**.
And all that *believed* **trusted** were *together* **in one**,
and had all *things* common;
And sold their possessions and goods,
and *parted* **divided** them to all *men*,
as every *man* **one** had need.
And they,
continuing daily *with one accord* **in unanimity**
in the *temple* **priestal precinct**,
and breaking bread from house to house
*did eat* **partook** their *meat* **nourishment**
*with gladness* **in jumping for joy**
and *singleness* **simplicity** of heart,
*Praising God* **Halaling Elohim**,
and having *favour* **charism** with all the people.
And *the Lord* **Adonay** added to the *church* **ecclesia** daily
such as should be saved.

# 117 Vignetes of

## ROSH HASHANA: ALSO KNOWN AS SEASON OF BLASTING, AND SEASON OF SHOPHAR

**Leviticus 23:23—25**

And *the LORD spake* **Yah Veh worded**
unto *Moses* **Mosheh**, saying,
*Speak* **Word** unto the *children* **sons** of *Israel* **Yisra El**,
saying,
In the seventh month, in the first *day* of the month,
shall ye have a *sabbath* **shabbathism**,
a memorial of *blowing of trumpets* **blasting**,
an holy convocation.
Ye shall *do* **work** no *servile* **service** work *therein*:
but ye shall *offer an offering made by fire* **oblate a firing**
unto *the LORD* **Yah Veh**.

• [7321] **teru'wah** *verb* clamor: whether blasting of shophars, clanging of cymbals, or shouting of persons.

**Psalm 118:24—26**

This is the day
*which the LORD* **Yah Veh** hath *made* **worked**;
we *will rejoice* **shall twirl** and *be glad* **cheer** in it.
Save now* **I beseech**,
I beseech thee, O *LORD* **Yah Veh**:
O *LORD* **Yah Veh**, I beseech thee,
*send now prosperity* **prosper, I beseech**.
Blessed be he
that cometh in the name of *the LORD* **Yah Veh**.

*Hoshia Nah

## NEW COVENANT FULFILLMENT

**Matthaios 21:5—111**

*Tell* **Say** ye the daughter of *Sion* **Siyon**,
Behold, thy *king* **sovereign** cometh unto thee,
meek, and *sitting* **mounted** upon *an ass* **a burro**,
and a colt the *foal* **son** of *an ass* **a burro**.
And the disciples went, and did **exactly**
as *Jesus commanded* **Yah Shua ordered** them,
And brought the *ass* **burro**, and the colt,
and put on them their *clothes* **garments**,
and they set him thereon.
And a *very great* **vast** multitude
extend their garments in the way;
others cut down branches from the trees,
and *strawed* **extend** them in the way.
And the multitudes that went before, and that followed,
cried, *saying* **wording**,
*Hosanna* **Hoshia Na** to the son of David:
*Blessed* **Eulogized** is he
that cometh in the name of *the Lord* **Yah Veh**;
*Hosanna* **Hoshia Na** in the *highest* **highests**.
And when he
*was come* **entered** into *Jerusalem* **Yeru Shalem**,
all the city *was moved* **quaked**, *saying* **wording**,
Who is this?
And the multitude *said* **worded**,
This is *Jesus* **Yah Shua**
the prophet of Nazareth of *Galilee* **Galiyl**.

## YAH SHUA CLEANSES THE PRIESTAL PRECINCT

**Matthaios 21:12—15**

And *Jesus went into* **Yah Shua entered**
the *temple* **priestal precinct** of *God* **Elohim**,
and *cast out* **ejected** all them that
sold and *bought* **marketed**
in the *temple* **priestal precinct**,
and *overthrew* **upset** the tables
of the *moneychangers* **coindealers**,
and the *seats* **cathedras** of them that sold doves,
And *said* **worded** unto them, It is *written* **scribed**,
My house shall be called the house of prayer;
but ye have made it a *den* **grotto** of *thieves* **robbers**.

## YAH SHUA CURES THE BLIND AND THE LAME

And the blind and the lame
came to him in the *temple* **priestal precinct**;
and he *healed* **cured** them.
And when the *chief* **arch** priests and scribes
saw the *wonderful things* **marvels** that he did,
and the *children* **lads** crying in the *temple* **priestal precinct**,
and *saying* **wording**,
*Hosanna* **Hoshia Na** to the son of David;
they *were sore displeased* **indignified**,

## THE FINAL SHOPHAR

**1 Thessalonians 4:13—17**

But I *would* **will that you** not
*have you to be ignorant* **be unknowing**, brethren,
concerning them which are asleep,
that ye sorrow not,
even **exactly** as *others* **the rest** which have no hope.
For if we *believe* **trust**
that *Jesus* **Yah Shua** died and rose *again*,
*even so* **thus** them also
which sleep *in Jesus* **through Yah Shua**
*will God* **shall Elohim** bring with him.
For this we *say* **word** unto you
*by* **in** the word of *the Lord* **Adonay**,
that we which are alive and *remain* **survive**
unto the coming of *the Lord* **Adonay**
shall *not prevent* **never no way precede** them
which are asleep.
For *the Lord* **Adonay** himself
shall descend from the heavens
*with* **in** a *shout* **summons**,
*with* **in** the voice of the archangel,
and *with* **in** the *trump* trumpet of *God* **Elohim**:
and the dead in *Christ* **Messiah** shall rise first:
Then we which are alive and *remain* **survive**
shall be *caught up together* **seized simultaneously**
with them in the clouds,
to meet *the Lord* **Adonay** in the air:
and *so* **thus** shall we ever be with *the Lord* **Adonay**.

# 119 Vignettes of

## SEASON OF YOM KIPPURIM

- [3117] **yom** *noun* day
- [3722] **kaphar** *verb* to atone
- [3725] **kipurim** *plural noun* atonements

**Leviticus 23:26—32**

And *the LORD spake* **Yah Veh worded**
unto *Moses* **Mosheh**, saying,
*Also* **Only** on the tenth *day* of this seventh month
*there* shall be *a day of atonement* **Yom Kippurim**:
it shall be an holy convocation unto you;
and ye shall *afflict* **humble** your souls,
and *offer an offering made by fire* **oblate a firing**
unto *the LORD* **Yah Veh**.
And ye shall *do* **work** no work in that same day:
for it is *a day of atonement* **Yom Kippurim**,
to *make an atonement* **kapar/atone for you**
*before the LORD* **at the face of Yah Veh** your *God* **Elohim**.
For whatsoever soul it be
that shall not be *afflicted* **humbled** in that same day,
he shall be cut off from among his people.
And whatsoever soul it be
that *doeth* **worketh** any work in that same day,
the same soul *will* **shall** destroy from among his people.
Ye shall *do* **work** no *manner of* work:
it shall be *a* **an eternal** statute *for ever*
throughout your generations
in all your *dwellings* **settlements**.

It shall be unto you
a *sabbath* **shabbath** of *rest* **shabbathism**,
and ye shall *afflict* **humble** your souls:
in the ninth *day* of the month at even,
from even unto even,
shall ye *celebrate* **shabbathize** your *sabbath* **shabbath**.

**Psalm 40:6—8**

Sacrifice and offering thou didst not desire;
mine ears hast thou *opened* **pierced**:
*burnt offering* **holocaust** and *sin offering* **for sin**
hast thou not *required* **asked**.
Then said I, *Lo* **Behold**, I come:
in the *volume* **roll** of the *book* **scroll**
it is *written* **inscribed** of me,
I delight to *do* **work** thy *will* **pleasure**,
O my *God* **Elohim**:
yea, thy *law* **torah** is within my *heart* **inwards**.

## ATONEMENT IN THE NEW COVENANT

**Hebrews 9:25—28**

Nor yet that he should offer himself often,
**exactly** as the *high* **arch** priest
entereth into the *holy place* **Holies** every year
*with* **in** blood of others;
*For then* **Otherwise** must he often have suffered
since the foundation of the *world* **cosmos**:
but now once
in the *end* **completion/shalom** of the *world* **eon**
hath he *appeared* **been manifest** to put away sin
*by* **through** the sacrifice of himself.
And **inasmuch** as it is *appointed* **laid out**
unto *men* **humanity** once to die,
but after this the judgment:
*So Christ* **Thus ha Mashiyach** was *once* offered **once**
to *bear* **offer** the sins of many;
and unto them that *look for* **await** him
shall he *appear* **be seen** the second *time*
*without* **apart from** sin unto salvation.

## THE YEAR BY YEAR SACRIFICES UNDER THE TORAH

**Hebrews 10:1—9**

For the *law* **torah** having a shadow
of **the** good *things* to come,
and not the very *image* **icon** of the *things* **substance**,
can never **ever** with those sacrifices
which they offered year by year *continually* **in perpetuity**
*make the comers thereunto perfect*
**complete/shalam them who come**.
*For then* **Otherwise**
*would* **should** they not
have *ceased* **ever paused** to be offered?
because that
the *worshippers* **liturgizers** once *purged* **purified**
should **not still** have had *no more* conscience of sins.
But in those *sacrifices*
there is a remembrance *again made* of sins every year.
For it is *not possible* **impossible**
that the blood of bulls and of goats
should *take away* **remove** sins.
*Wherefore* **So** when he cometh into the *world* **cosmos**,
he *saith* **wordeth**,
Sacrifice and offering thou *wouldest* **willest** not,
but a body hast thou prepared me:
In *burnt offerings* **holocausts** and *sacrifices* for sin
thou hast *had no pleasure* **not thought well**.
Then said I, *Lo* **Behold**, I come
(in the *volume* **heading** of the *book* **scroll**
it is *written of* **scribed concerning** me,)
to do thy will, O *God* **Elohim**.
Above when he *said* **worded**,
Sacrifice and offering
and *burnt offerings* **holocausts** and *offering* for sin
thou *wouldest* **willest** not,
neither hadst *pleasure therein* **thought well**;
which are offered by the *law* **torah**;

## SEASON OF SUKKOTH: ALSO KNOWN AS BRUSH ARBORS. THE FEAST OF TABERNACLES AND THE FEAST OF BOOTHS

- [2282] **chag** *noun* celebration
- [5521] **sukkah** *noun* sokkoth *plural noun* a brush arbor — not a tabernacle or tent. You'll see why when we get to the Shechinah Glory!
- [5520] **cok** *noun* brush arbor
- [5526] **cakak** *verb* entwine

**Leviticus 23:33—38**

And *the LORD spake* **Yah Veh worded**
unto *Moses* **Mosheh,** saying,
*Speak* **Word** unto the *children* **sons** of *Israel* **Yisra El**,
saying,
The fifteenth day of this seventh month
shall be the *feast* **celebration**
of *tabernacles* **sukkoth/brush arbors**
for seven days unto *the LORD* **Yah Veh**.
On the first day shall be an holy convocation:
ye shall *do* **work** no *servile* **service** work *therein*.
Seven days ye shall
*offer an offering made by fire* **oblate a firing**
unto *the LORD* **Yah Veh**:
on the eighth day shall be an holy convocation unto you;
and ye shall *offer an offering made by fire* **oblate a firing**
unto *the LORD* **Yah Veh**:
it is a *solemn assembly* **an abstinence**;
and ye shall *do* **work** no *servile* **service** work *therein*.
These are the *feasts* **seasons** of *the LORD* **Yah Veh**,
which ye shall *proclaim* **recall** to be holy convocations,
to *offer an offering made by fire* **oblate a firing**
unto *the LORD* **Yah Veh**,
a *burnt offering* **holocaust**, and *a meat* **an** offering,
a sacrifice, and *drink offerings* **libations**,
every *thing upon his day* **word day by day**:
Beside the *sabbaths* **shabbaths** of *the LORD* **Yah Veh**,
and beside your gifts, and beside all your vows,
and beside all your *freewill offerings* **voluntaries**,
which ye give unto *the LORD* **Yah Veh**.

Some of my octagenarian friends may well remember the Brush Arbor meetings held in the southland before tent meetings became popular.

And I suppose some of my fellows feel that the Brush Arbor meetings were more spiritual than the Tent meetings.

The Brush Arbor differs from the Tabernacle and is not to be thought of as the same.

The Brush Arbor Celebration was for a Harvest Time Celebration, whereas the Tent which covered the Tabernacle was specifically a Worship Center.

Some theologians say that Shua was birthed in a Brush Arbor, rather than in a crib.

## THE SHABBATHISM OF BRUSH ARBORS

- [7673] **shabbath** *verb* to cease from exertion
- [7676] **shabbath** *noun* a time to cease from exertion.
- [7677] **shabbathon** *noun* a ceasing from exertion.

**Leviticus 23:39—44**

Also in the fifteenth day of the seventh month,
when ye have gathered in the *fruit* **produce** of the land,
ye shall *keep* **celebrate** a *feast* **celebration**
unto *the LORD* **Yah Veh** seven days:
on the first day shall be a *sabbath* **shabbathism**,
and on the eighth day shall be a *sabbath* **shabbathism**.
And ye shall take you on the first day
the boughs of *goodly* **majestic** trees,
*branches* **palms** of palm trees,
and the *boughs* **fruit** of thick trees,
and willows of the *brook* **wadi**;
and ye shall *rejoice* **cheer**
*before the LORD* **at the face of Yah Veh** your *God* **Elohim**
seven days.

And ye shall *keep it* **celebrate** a *feast* **celebration**
unto *the LORD* **Yah Veh** seven days in the year.
It shall be a **an eternal** statute *for ever* in your generations:
ye shall celebrate it in the seventh month.
Ye shall *dwell* **sit** in *booths* **sukkoth/brush arbors**
seven days;
all that are *Israelites born* **Yisra Eliy birthed**
shall *dwell* **sit** in *booths* **sukkoth/brush arbors**:
That your generations may know
that I *made* **caused** the *children* **sons** of *Israel* **Yisra El**
to *dwell* **sit** in *booths* **sukkoth/brush arbors**,
when I brought them out of the land of *Egypt* **Misrayim**:
*I am the LORD* **I — Yah Veh** your *God* **Elohim**.
And *Moses declared* **Mosheh worded**
unto the *children* **sons** of *Israel* **Yisra El**

**Isn't Yah Veh good? So sit in the shade, celebrate your harvest, relax. Imagine! After all your celebrating, he desires that you take it easy. What a life?!**

## SEASON OF CHANUKKAH MISNAMED THE FESTIVAL OF LIGHTS AND CHRISTMAS

Chanukkah and Christmas are now desecrations of Elohim's intended purpose. Instead of being a celebration of hallowing, Chanukkah and Christmas have become a festival of lights.

There are Rabbi's and Theologians who are unaware that Chanukkah is a transliteration in the Old Covenant and a mistranslation in the new.

• [2596] **chanu** *transliterated verb* chanukkah to celebrate a hallowing.

**Proverbs 22:6**

*Train up a child* **Chanukkah a lad by mouth**
*in the way he should go* **about his way**:
and when he *is old* **ageth**,
he *will* **shall** not *depart* **turn aside** from it.

## NEWLYWEDS DON'T GO TO WAR

**Deuteronomy 20:1—5**

When thou goest out to *battle* **war**
against thine enemies,
and seest horses, and chariots,
and a people more than thou,
*be not afraid of* **awe** them **not**:
for *the LORD* **Yah Veh** thy *God* **Elohim** is with thee,
which *brought* **ascended** thee *up*
out of the land of *Egypt* **Misrayim**.
And it shall be,
when ye *are come nigh* **approach** unto the *battle* **war**,
that the priest shall approach
and *speak* **word** unto the people,
And shall say unto them, Hear, O *Israel* **Yisra El**,
ye approach this day unto battle against your enemies:
let not your hearts *faint* **tenderize**,
*fear* **awe** not, and do not *tremble* **hasten**,
neither be ye terrified *because of them* **at their face**;
For *the LORD* **Yah Veh** your *God* **Elohim**
is he that goeth with you,
to fight for you against your enemies, to save you.
And the officers shall *speak* **word** unto the people,
saying, What man is there that hath built a new house,
and hath not *dedicated* **chanukkahed** it?
let him go and return to his house,
lest he die in the *battle* **war**,
and another man *dedicate* **chanukkah** it.

## THE CHANUKKAH OF THE HOUSE OF YAH VEH

**2 Chronicles 7:1—9**

Now when *Solomon* **Shelomoh**
had *made an end of* **finished** praying,
the fire *came down* **descended** from *heaven* **the heavens**,
and consumed
the *burnt offering* **holocaust** and the sacrifices;
and the glory of *the LORD* **Yah Veh** filled the house.
And the priests could not enter
into the house of *the LORD* **Yah Veh**,
because the glory of *the LORD* **Yah Veh**
had filled the *LORD'S* house **of Yah Veh**.
And when all the *children* **sons** of *Israel* **Yisra El**
saw how the fire *came down* **descended**,
and the glory of *the LORD* **Yah Veh** upon the house,
they bowed themselves
with their *faces* **nostrils** to the *ground* **earth**
upon the pavement, and *worshipped* **prostrated**,
and *praised the LORD* **spread hands to Yah Veh**,
saying, For he is good;
for his mercy *endureth for ever* **eternal**.
Then the *king* **sovereign** and all the people
*offered* **sacrificed** sacrifices
*before the LORD* **at the face of Yah Veh**.
And *king Solomon* **sovereign Shelomoh**
*offered* **sacrificed** a sacrifice
of twenty and two thousand oxen,
and an hundred and twenty thousand *sheep* **flocks**:
so the *king* **sovereign** and all the people
*dedicated* **chanukkahed** the house of *God* **Elohim**.
And the priests *waited* **stood** on their *offices* **guards**:
the *Levites* **Leviym** also with instruments of *musick* **song**
of *the LORD* **Yah Veh**,
which David the *king* **sovereign** had *made* **worked**
to *praise the LORD* **spread hands to Yah Veh**,
*because* **for** his mercy *endureth for ever* **is eternal**,
when David *praised* **halaled** by their *ministry* **hand**;
and the priests *sounded* **trumpeted** trumpets before them,
and all *Israel* **Yisra El** stood.
*Moreover Solomon* **Shelomoh**
hallowed the middle of the court
*that was before* **at the face of** the house of *the LORD* **Yah Veh**:
for there he *offered burnt offerings* **worked holocausts**,
and the fat of the *peace offerings* **shelamim**,
because the *brasen* **copper sacrifice** altar
which *Solomon* **Shelomoh** had *made* **worked**
was not able to *receive* **contain**
the *burnt offerings* **holocausts**,
and the *meat* offerings, and the fat.
Also at the same time *Solomon* **Shelomoh**
*kept* **worked** the *feast* **celebration** seven days,
and all *Israel* **Yisra El** with him,
a *very* **mighty** great congregation,
from the entering in of Hamath
unto the *river* **wadi** of *Egypt* **Misrayim**.
And in the eighth day
they *made* **worked** a *solemn* **private** assembly:
for they *kept* **worked** the *dedication* **chanukkah**
of the **sacrifice** altar seven days,
and the *feast* **celebration** seven days.

# 125 Vignettes of

## THE CHANUKKAH OF THE HOUSE OF YAH VEH

**1 Sovereigns 8:62, 63**
And the *king* **sovereign**, and all *Israel* **Yisra El** with him,
*offered* **sacrificed** sacrifice
*before the LORD* **at the face of Yah Veh**.
And *Solomon offered* **Shelomoh sacrificed**
a sacrifice of *peace offerings* **shelamim**,
which he *offered* **sacrificed** unto *the LORD* **Yah Veh**,
two and twenty thousand oxen,
and an hundred and twenty thousand *sheep* **flocks**.
So the *king* **sovereign**
and all the *children* **sons** of *Israel* **Yisra El**
*dedicated* **chanukkahed** the house of *the LORD* **Yah Veh**.

## CHANUKKAH OF THE HOUSE OF ELAH*

• [2597] (Aramaic) **chanukkah** *transliterated noun*
chanukkah: a celebration of hallowing.

**Ezra 6:16, 17**
And the *children* **sons** of *Israel* **Yisra El**,
the priests, and the *Levites* **Leviym**,
and the *rest* **survivors**
of the *children* **sons** of the *captivity* **exile**,
kept the *dedication* **chanukkah** of this house of *God* **Elah**
with *joy* **rejoicing**.
And *offered* **oblated** at the *dedication* **chanukkah**
of this house of *God* **Elah**:
an hundred *bullocks* **bulls**,
two hundred rams, four hundred lambs;
and for *a sin offering* **the sin** for all *Israel* **Yisra El**,
twelve *he goats* **buck goats of the doe goats**,
according to the *number* **enumeration**
of the *tribes* **scions** of *Israel* **Yisra El**.

*Elah: Aramaic for Eloh (singular)

## THE CHANUKKAH OF THE SACRIFICE ALTAR

• [2598] (Hebrew) **chanukkah** *transliterated noun*
chanukkah: a celebration of hallowing.

**Numbers 7:10, 11**
And the *princes offered* **hierarchs oblated**
for *dedicating* **the chanukkah** of the **sacrifice** altar
in the day that it was anointed,
even the *princes* **hierarchs**
*offered* **oblated** their *offering* **qorban**
*before the* **at the face of the sacrifice** altar.
And *the LORD* **Yah Veh** said unto *Moses* **Mosheh**,
They shall *offer* **oblate** their *offering* **qorban**,
*each prince on his day*
**one hierarch a day — one hierarch a day**,
for the *dedicating* **chanukkah** of the **sacrifice** altar.

**Numbers 7:84—89**
This was the *dedicating* **chanukkah** of the sacrifice altar,
in the day when it was anointed,
by the *princes* **hierarchs** of *Israel* **Yisra El**:
twelve *chargers* **dishes** of silver,
twelve silver *bowls* **sprinklers**, twelve spoons of gold:
Each *charger* **dish** of silver
weighing an hundred and thirty shekels,
each *bowl* **sprinkler** seventy:
all the silver *vessels* **instruments** weighed
two thousand and four hundred *shekels*,
after the shekel of the sanctuary holies:
The golden *spoons* **bowls** were twelve, full of incense,
*weighing ten shekels apiece* **each bowl, ten, ten,**
after the shekel of the sanctuary holies:
all the gold of the *spoons* **bowls**
was an hundred and twenty *shekels*.
All the oxen for the **burnt offering** holocaust
were twelve bullocks, the rams twelve,
the lambs *of the first year* **yearling sons** twelve,
with their *meat* offering:
and the *kids* **bucks** of the goats for *sin offering* **for the sin**
twelve.
And all the oxen
for the sacrifice of the *peace offerings* **shelamim**
were twenty and four bullocks,
the rams sixty, the he goats sixty,
the lambs *of the first year* **yearling sons** sixty.
This was the *dedicating* **chanukkah** of the **sacrifice** altar,
after that it was anointed.
And when *Moses* **Mosheh**
was gone into the *tabernacle* **tent** of the congregation
to *speak* **word** with him,
then he heard the voice of one *speaking* **wording** unto him
from off the *mercy seat* **kapporeth**
that was upon the ark of *testimony* **witness**,
from between the two *cherubims* **cherubim**:
and he spake **worded** unto him.

## THE PSALM OF THE CHANUKKAH OF THE HOUSE OF DAVID

**Psalm 30:1—12**

A Psalm and Song
at the *dedication* **chanukkah** of the house of David.
I *will extol* **shall exalt** thee, O *LORD* **Yah Veh**;
for thou hast *lifted* **bailed** me up,
and hast not made my *foes* **enemies**
to *rejoice* **cheer** over me.
O *LORD* **Yah Veh** my *God* **Elohim**,
I cried unto thee, and thou hast healed me.
O *LORD* **Yah Veh**,
thou hast *brought up* **ascended** my soul
from *the grave* **sheol**:
thou hast *kept me alive* **enlivened me**,
that I should not *go down* **descend** to the *pit* **well**.
*Sing* **Psalm** unto *the LORD* **Yah Veh**,
O ye *saints* **mercied** of his,
and *give thanks* **spread hands**
at the *remembrance* **memorial** of his holiness.
For his *anger endureth* **wrath is** but a *moment* **blink**;
in his *favour* **pleasure** is life:
weeping may *endure* **stay** for *a night* **an evening**,
but *joy cometh* **shouting** in the morning.

And in my *prosperity* **serenity** I said,
I shall *never be moved* **not totter eternally**.
O *LORD* **Yah Veh**, by thy *favour* **pleasure**
thou hast made my mountain
to stand *strong* **in strength**:
thou *didst hide* **hid** thy face, and I was *troubled* **terrified**.
I *cried* **called** to thee, O *LORD* **Yah Veh**;
and unto *the LORD* **Yah Veh**
I *made supplication* **sought charism**.
What *profit* **gain** is there in my blood,
when I *go down* **descend** to the pit **of ruin**?
Shall the dust *praise* **spread hands unto** thee?
shall it *declare* **tell** thy truth?
Hear, O *LORD* **Yah Veh**,
and *have mercy upon me* **grant me charism**:
O *LORD* **Yah Veh**, be thou my helper.
Thou hast turned for me
my *mourning* **chopping** into **round** dancing:
thou hast *put off* **loosed** my *sackcloth* **saq**,
and girded me with *gladness* **cheerfullness**;
*To the end* that my glory may *sing praise* **psalm** to thee
and not *be silent* **hush**.
O *LORD* **Yah Veh** my *God* **Elohim**,
I *will give thanks* **shall spread hands** unto thee
*for ever* **eternally**.

## CHANUKKAH OF THE WALL OF YERU SHALEM

**Nechem Yah 12:27**

And at the *dedication* **chanukkah**
of the wall of *Jerusalem* **Yeru Shalem**
they sought the *Levites* **Leviym** out of all their places,
to bring them to *Jerusalem* **Yeru Shalem**,
to *keep* **work** the *dedication* **chanukkah**
with *gladness* **cheer**,
both with *thanksgivings* **spread hands**, and with singing,
with cymbals, *psalteries* **bagpipes**, and with harps.

## CHANUKKAH OF THE IMAGE OF GOLD OF NEBUKADNETZ TZAR

**Dani El 3:1—3**

*NEBUCHADNEZZAR* **Nebukadnets Tsar**
the *king* **sovereign** made an image of gold,
whose height was *threescore* **sixty** cubits,
and the breadth *thereof* six cubits:
he *set it up* **raised it** in the *plain* **valley** of Dura,
in the *province* **jurisdiction** of *Babylon* **Babel**.

Then *Nebuchadnezzar* **Nebukadnets Tsar**
the *king* **sovereign**
sent to gather together the *princes* **satraps**,
the *governors* **prefects**, and the *captains* **governors**,
the *judges* **mighty diviners**, the treasurers,
the *counsellors* **decreers**, the sherriffs,
and all the *rulers* **dominators** of the *provinces* **jurisdictions**,
to come to the *dedication* **chanukkah** of the image
which *Nebuchadnezzar* **Nebukadnets Tsar**
the *king* **sovereign** had *set up* **raised**.
Then the *princes* **satraps**, the *governors* **prefects**,
and *captains* **governors**, the *judges* **mighty diviners**,
the treasurers, the counsellors, the sheriffs,
and all the *rulers* **dominators**
of the *provinces* **jurisdictions**
were gathered together
unto the *dedication* **chanukkah** of the image
that *Nebuchadnezzar* **Nebukadnets Tsar**
the *king* **sovereign** had *set up* **raised**;
and they *stood before* **rose in front of** the image
that *Nebuchadnezzar* **Nebukadnets Tsar**
had *set up* **raised**.

## CHANUKKAH IN THE NEW COVENANT

- {1456} **enkainia** *noun* chanukkah: a celebration of hallowing.
- {1457} **enkainizo** *verb* to chanukkah: to celebrate a hallowing.

## YAH SHUA, HA MASCHIYACH

**Yah Chanan 10:22—24**

And it *was* **became** at *Jerusalem* **Yeru Shalem**
the *feast of the dedication* **chanukkah**,
and it was *winter* **the downpour**.
And *Jesus* **Yah Shua**
walked in the *temple* **priestal precinct**
in *Solomon's porch* **Shelomoh's portico**.
*Then came* **So** the *Jews* **Yah Hudiym**
*round about* **surrounded him**, and *said* **worded** unto him,
*How long* **Until when**
dost thou *make us to doubt* **lift our soul in suspense**?
If thou be the *Christ* **ha Mashiyach**,
*tell* **say to** us *plainly* **boldly**.

## THE COSMIC HOLY TABERNACLE

### Hebrews 9:1—16

*Then verily* **But indeed** the first *covenant* **tabernacle**
had also
*ordinances* **judgments** of *divine service* **ministration**,
and a *worldly sanctuary* **cosmic Holies**.
For there was a tabernacle *made* **prepared**;
the first, wherein was the *candlestick* **menorah**,
and the table, and the *shewbread* **prothesis bread**;
which is *called* **worded** the *sanctuary* **Holies**.
And after the second veil, the tabernacle
which is *called* **worded** the *Holiest of all* **Holy of Holies**;
Which had the golden *censer* **incenser**,
and the ark of the covenant
*overlaid round* **covered** about **on every side** with gold,
wherein was the golden *pot* **jar** that had manna,
and *Aaron's rod* **Aharon's scion** that *budded* **sprouted**,
and the *tables* **slabs** of the covenant;

And over it the *cherubims* **cherubim** of glory
shadowing the *mercyseat* **kapporeth**;
*of* **about** which we cannot now *speak* **word**
*particularly* **according to its parts**.
Now when these *things* were thus *ordained* **prepared**,
the priests **indeed**
*went always into* **continually entered** the first tabernacle,
*accomplishing* **fully completing**
the *service of God* **liturgy**.
But into the second
went the *high* **arch** priest alone once every year,
not *without* **apart from** blood,
which he offered for himself,
and *for* **the** *errors* **unknowingnesses** of the people:
The Holy *Ghost* **Spirit** this *signifying* **evidencing**,
that the way into the *holiest of all* **Holies**
was not yet *made* manifest,
while as the first tabernacle was yet standing:
Which was a *figure* **parable**
*for the time* **unto that season** then present,
in which were offered both *gifts* **gratuities** and sacrifices,

that could not *make* **complete/shalam** him
that *did the service perfect* **liturgized**,
as pertaining to the conscience;
*Which stood* only *in meats* **upon food** and drinks,
and *divers washings* **more excellent baptisms**,
and *carnal ordinances* **judgments of flesh**,
imposed *on them* until
the *time* **season** of *reformation* **thorough straightening**.
But *Christ* **ha Mashiyach** being come,
an *high* **arch** priest of **the coming** good *things to come*,
*by* **through** a greater
and *more perfect* **completed/shalamed** tabernacle,
not *made with hands* **handmade**,
that is *to say*, not of this *building* **creation**;
Neither *by* **through** the blood of goats and calves,
but *by* **through** his own blood
he entered in once into the *holy place* **Holies**,
having *obtained* **found** eternal redemption *for us*.
For if the blood of bulls and of goats,
and the ashes of an heifer sprinkling the *unclean* **profane**,
*sanctifieth* **halloweth** to the purifying of the flesh:
How much more shall the blood of *Christ* **ha Mashiyach**,
who through the eternal Spirit offered himself
*without spot* **unblemished** to *God* **Elohim**,

*purge* **purify** your conscience from dead works
to *serve* **liturgize** the living *God* **Elohim**?
And *for this cause* **which**
he is the mediator of the new *testament* **covenant**,
that *by means of* **having become by** death,
*for* **unto** the redemption of the transgressions
*that were* under the first *testament* **covenant**,
they which are called
might *receive* **take** the *promise* **pre—evangelism**
of eternal inheritance.
For where a *testament* **covenant** is,
there must also of necessity
be **brought** the death of the *testator* **covenantor**.
For a *testament* **covenant** is *of force* **stedfast**
*after men are dead* **upon death**:
otherwise it is *of no strength* **not mighty enough** at all
while the *testator* **covenantor** liveth.
*Whereupon* **And so**
neither the first *testament* was *dedicated* **chanukkahed**
*without* **apart from** blood.
For when *Moses* **Mosheh**
had spoken every *precept* **misvah**
to all the people according to the *law* **torah**,

he took the blood of calves and of goats,
with water, and scarlet wool, and hyssop,
and sprinkled both the *book* **scroll**,
and all the people,
*Saying* **Wording**,
This is the blood of the *testament* **covenant**
which *God* **Yah Veh** hath *enjoined* **misvahed** unto you.
*Moreover* **Likewise** he sprinkled with blood
both the tabernacle,
and all the vessels of the *ministry* **liturgy**.
And *almost* **nearly** all *things* are,
*by* **according to** the *law* **torah,**
*purged with* **purified in** blood;
and *without shedding* **apart from pouring** of blood
*is no remission* **becometh no forgiveness**.
**So indeed** It was *therefore* necessary
that the *patterns of things* **examples** in the heavens
should be purified with these;
but the *heavenly things* **heavenlies** themselves
with better sacrifices than these.
For *Christ* **ha Mashiyach** is not entered into
the *holy places made with hands* **handmade Holies**,
*which are the figures* **antitypes** of the true;
but into *heaven* **the heavens** itself,
now to *appear* **manifest**
in the *presence* **face** of *God* **Elohim** for us:
Nor yet that he should offer himself often,
**exactly** as the *high* **arch** priest
entereth into the *holy place* **Holies** every year
*with* **in** blood of others;
*For then* **Otherwise** must he often have suffered
since the foundation of the *world* **cosmos**:
but now once
in the *end* **completion/shalom** of the *world* **eon**
hath he *appeared* **been manifest** to put away sin
*by* **through** the sacrifice of himself.
And **inasmuch** as it is *appointed* **laid out**
unto *men* **humanity** once to die,
but after this the judgment:
*So Christ* **Thus ha Mashiyach** was *once* offered **once**
to *bear* **offer** the sins of many;
and unto them that *look for* **await** him
shall he *appear* **be seen** the second *time*
*without* **apart from** sin unto salvation.

## THE YEAR BY YEAR SACRIFICES UNDER THE TORAH

**Hebrews 10:1—25**

For the *law* **torah** having a shadow
of **the coming** good *things to come*,
and not the very *image* **icon** of the *things* **substance**,
can never **ever** with those sacrifices
which they offered year by year *continually* **in perpetuity**
*make the comers thereunto perfect*
**complete/shalam them who come**.
*For then* **Otherwise**
*would* **should** they not
have *ceased* **ever paused** to be offered?
because that
the *worshippers* **liturgizers** once *purged* **purified**
should **not still** have had *no more* conscience of sins.
But in those *sacrifices*
there is a remembrance *again made* of sins every year.
For it is *not possible* **impossible**
that the blood of bulls and of goats
should *take away* **remove** sins.
*Wherefore* **So** when he cometh into the *world* **cosmos**,
he *saith* **wordeth**,
Sacrifice and offering thou *wouldest* **willest** not,
but a body hast thou prepared me:
In *burnt offerings* **holocausts** and *sacrifices* for sin
thou hast *had no pleasure* **not thought well**.
Then said I, *Lo* **Behold**, I come
(in the *volume* **heading** of the *book* **scroll**
it is *written of* **scribed concerning** me,)
to do thy will, O *God* **Elohim**.
Above when he *said* **worded**,
Sacrifice and offering
and *burnt offerings* **holocausts** and *offering* for sin
thou *wouldest* **willest** not,
neither hadst *pleasure therein* **thought well**;
which are offered by the *law* **torah**;
Then said he, *Lo* **Behold**,
I come to do thy will, O *God* **Elohim**.
He taketh away the first,
that he may *establish* **set** the second.
*By the* **In** which will we are *sanctified* **hallowed**
through the offering
of the body of *Jesus Christ* **Yah Shua ha Mashiyach**
once *for all*.
And every priest **indeed** standeth daily
*ministering* **liturgizing** and offering
*oftentimes* the same sacrifices **often**,
which can never **ever** take away sins:

## THE SACRIFICE OF THE SON — ONCE

But this *man* **one**,
after he had offered one sacrifice for sins
*for ever* **in perpetuity**,

sat down *on* **at** the right *hand* of *God* **Elohim**;
From henceforth *expecting* **awaiting**
till his enemies be *made* **placed** his footstool.
For by one offering he hath
*perfected for ever* **completed/shalamed in perpetuity**
them that are *sanctified* **hallowed**.
*Whereof* the Holy *Ghost* **Spirit** also
*is a witness* **witnesseth** to us:
for after that he had *said before* **foretold**,
This is the covenant
that I *will make* **shall covenant** with them
after those days,
*saith the Lord* **wordeth Yah Veh**,
I *will put* **shall give** my *laws* **torah** into their hearts,
and in their minds *will I write* **shall I epigraph** them;
And their sins and *iniquities* **torah violations**
*will I* **shall I not no way still** remember *no more*.
Now where *remission* **forgiveness** of these is,
there is *no more* **not still** offering for sin.
**So** Having *therefore*, brethren,
boldness to enter into the *holiest* **Holies**
*by* **in** the blood of *Jesus* **Yah Shua**,
By a *new* **freshly slaughtered** and living way,
which he hath *consecrated* **chanukkahed** for us,
through the veil, that is *to say*, his flesh;
And having *an high* **a mega** priest
over the house of *God* **El**;

Let us *draw* **come** near with a true heart
in full *assurance* **bearance** of *faith* **trust**,
having our hearts sprinkled from an evil conscience,
and our bodies *washed* **bathed** with pure water.
Let us hold *fast* **down** the profession of *our faith* **hope**
*without wavering* **unwaveringly**;
(for he is *faithful* **trustworthy**
that *promised* **pre—evangelized**;)
And let us consider one another
to *provoke* **agitate** unto love and to good works:
Not forsaking
the *assembling* **synagoguing** of ourselves together,
**exactly** as the *manner* **custom** of some is;
but *exhorting one another* **consoling**:
and so much the more,
as **long as** ye see the day approaching.

~ ~~

## A CHANUKKAH CHRISTMAS BIRTHDAY TUNE

Happy Chanukkah to you,
Happy Chanukkah to you;
Happy Chanukkah Yah Shua ha Mashiyach,
Happy Chanukkah to you.
— and many more.

# 135 Vignettes of

## THE TEN WORDS OF ELOHIM

**Exodus 20:1—17** And Elohim worded all these words, saying, I am Yah Veh thy Elohim, which have brought thee out of the land of Mizrayim, out of the house of servitude.

There shall be no other elohim at my face.

Work not any sculptile, or any similitude of aught that is in the heavens above, or that is in the earth beneath, or that is in the water beneath the earth: Neither prostrate thyself to them, nor serve them: for I Yah Veh thy Elohim am a jealous El, visiting the perversity of the fathers upon the sons unto the third and fourth generation of them that hate me; And working mercy unto thousands of them that love me, and guard my mizvoth.

Lift not the name of Yah Veh thy Elohim in defamation; for Yah Veh shall not exonerate him that lifteth his name in defamation.

Remember the shabbath day, to hallow it. Six days shalt thou serve, and work all thy work: But the seventh day is the shabbath of Yah Veh thy Elohim: in it thou shalt not work any work, thou, or thy son, or thy daughter, thy servant, or thy maid, or thy animals, or thy sojourner that is within thy gates: For in six days Yah Veh worked the heavens and earth, the sea, and all that in them is, and rested the seventh day: wherefore Yah Veh blessed the shabbath day, and hallowed it.

Honour thy father and thy mother: that thy days may be prolonged upon the soil which Yah Veh thy Elohim giveth thee.

Murder not.

Adulterize not.

Steal not.

Answer not a false witness against thy friend.

Thou shalt not desire thy friend's house, thou shalt not desire thy friend's woman, or his servant, or his maid, nor or his ox, or his burro, or aught that is thy friend's.

# Ten Words 136

It has been said, "The Bible throws great light on the commentaries." And in my ministry, I have avoided expanding and opining — and now, I beseech, allow me to ramble a wee bit.

Ramble one: Of all the mizvoth (commandments) Yah Veh has instructed, I wonder why Scripture states, quite simple, "He worded these words."

Ramble two: As you now go back (go back, I'll wait) and reread these ten words, ask yourself:

1. Which word is the easiest to guard?
2. Which word is kinda' tough?
3. Which word am I sort of ignoring?

Would it possibly be the word Yah Veh invests most of his words on?

I'm not senile, though I may be senescing a bit, but having translated and transliterated every word of Scripture, I do not remember every word I researched.

So when I visited some of the congregations who were endorsing the exeGeses Bibles, I discovered that, because of its accuracy, the exeGeses Bible surmounted denominational bounds.

When I first visited Messianic Congregtions, I discovered that I had translated 'The Feast Days' accurately — and that I had translated some in the New Covenant of which some of the Rabbis had not been aware.

And even though I had been, what the world calls, a 'Christian' for sixty—five years, it was not until I began my work that I discovered that 'Jesus Christ' meant 'Yah Shua ha Mashiyach' — the 'Anointed Eternal saviour'.

Are you prepared for an adventure?

Ere we begin to assimilate the possibilities of these ten words that Yah Veh worded, let's assess our present "where we are" opinions.

So get a pen, turn the page, and get ready for a big surprise.

# 137 Vignettes of

**OPINION SURVEY**

Everybody loves a survey — especially when we only give our opinion. Give your opinion on the following:

1. There shall be no other elohim at my face.

2. Work not any sculptile, or any similitude of aught that is in the heavens above, or that is in the earth beneath, or that is in the water beneath the earth: Neither prostrate thyself to them, nor serve them:

   What would you include under sculptile?

3. Lift not the name of Yah Veh thy Elohim in defamation.

   What does 'lift' mean to you?

   Does it include naming the name?

4. Honour thy father and thy mother.

5 Murder not.

   Does murder include self defense? War?

6. Adulterize not.
What part of 'not' do you not understand?

7. Steal not.

8. Answer not a false witness against thy friend.

9. Thou shalt not desire thy friend's house, thou shalt not desire thy friend's woman, or his servant, or his maid, nor or his ox, or his burro, or aught that is thy friend's.

All of a sudden we are getting into detail — to which some would say, "That's a very personal matter."

10. Remember the Shabbath day to hallow it.

Last (in our listing) but not least, but perhaps the least understood.

Are we to worship 'on the Shabbath', or
Are we to worship 'the Shabbath'?

End of SURVEY!

# 139 Vignettes of

## A CHANGING WORLD IN CHANGING TIMES WITH A NON—CHANGING ELOHIM!

One of the many common expressions expressed by expressionists is, "Well, it's not carved in stone" — meaning that we can change it at any time to suit our personal needs and desires.

Allow me to state this: The ten words worded to Mosheh were carved in stone — twice — by the finger of Elohim.

**Exodus 31:18**

And he gave unto Mosheh, when he had finished wording with him upon mount Siyniy, two slabs of witness, slabs of stone scribed with the finger of Elohim.

The first memory lesson of so many of us was to recite the Ten Words. In our times of maturation, we sorta' slipped over the ones on portraying and/or wearing sculptiles — whether fish, cross, or crucifix — and really (and I hate the word, 'really' — I really do) 'winked at' guarding the Shabbath — some even calling the first day the Shabbath.

No matter what your convictions, or lack of them, I plead with you that have an open heart (without any surgery) to the Scriptures on Shabbath.

## WORD STUDIES ON SHABBATH

- [7673] **shabbath** *verb* to shabbathize: to cease from exertion and to hallow.
- [7676] **shabbath** *noun* a time to cease from exertion and to hallow.
- [7677] **shabbathon** *noun* a ceasing from exertion and a hallowing.
- {4315} **prosabbaton** *noun* pre—shabbath only in Markos 15:42
- {4521} **sabbaton**, **sabbata**

The first mention of Shabbath is in its verbal form after Elohim had had a very busy week:

**Genesis 2:1—3**

*Thus* the heavens and the earth were finished,
and all the host of them.
And on the seventh day
*God ended* **Elohim finished** his work
which he had *made* **worked**;
and he *rested* **shabbathized** [7673] on the seventh day
from all his work which he had *made* **worked**.
And *God* **Elohim** blessed the seventh day,
and *sanctified* **hallowed** it:
because that in it
he had *rested* **shabbathized** [7673] from all his work
which *God* **Elohim** created and *made* **worked**.

The following verse presents two words from the root of Shabbath:

**Exodus 16:23**

And he said unto them,
This is that which *the LORD* **Yah Veh** hath *said* **worded**,
To morrow is the *rest* **shabbathism** [7677]
of the holy *sabbath* **shabbath** [7676]
unto *the LORD* **Yah Veh**:
bake that which ye *will* **shall** bake *to day*,
and *seethe* **stew** that ye *will seethe* **shall stew**;
and *that which remaineth over* **all the leftovers**
*lay up* **leave** for you to be *kept* **guarded** until the morning

## The SHABBATH IS A SIGN BETWEEN ELOHIM AND BETWEEN HUMANITY

**Exodus 31:12—17**

And *the LORD spake* **Yah Veh worded**
unto *Moses* **Mosheh**, saying,
*Speak* **Word** thou also
unto the *children* **sons** of *Israel* **Yisra El**, saying,
*Verily* **Surely** my *sabbaths* **shabbaths** [7676}
ye shall *keep* **guard**:
for it is a sign between me and **between** you
throughout your generations;
that ye may know that *I am the LORD* **I — Yah Veh**
that *doth sanctify* **halloweth** you.
Ye shall *keep* **guard** the *sabbath* **shabbath** [7676} therefore;
for it is holy unto you:
every one that *defileth* **profaneth** it,
**in being deathified,**
shall *surely be put to death* **be deathified**:
for whosoever *doeth any* **worketh** work therein,
that soul shall be cut off from among his people.
Six days may work be *done* **worked**;
*but in* the seventh **day**
is the *sabbath* **shabbath** [7676} of *rest* **shabbathism** [7677},
holy to *the LORD* **Yah Veh**:
whosoever *doeth any* **worketh** work
in the *sabbath* **shabbath** [7676} day,
**in being deathified,**
he shall *surely be put to death* **be deathified**.
*Wherefore* the *children* **sons** of *Israel* **Yisra El**
shall *keep* **guard** the *sabbath* **shabbath** [7676},
to *observe* **work** the *sabbath* **shabbath** [7676}
throughout their generations,
for *a perpetual* **an eternal** covenant.
It is a sign between me
and **between** the *children* **sons** of *Israel* **Yisra El**
*for ever* **eternally**:
for in six days *the LORD* **Yah Veh**
*made heaven* **worked the heavens** and earth,
and on the seventh day he *rested* **shabbathized**,
and *was refreshed* **exhaled**.
And he gave unto *Moses* **Mosheh**,
when he had
*made an end of communing* **finished wording**
with him upon mount *Sinai* **Sinay**,
two *tables* **slabs** of *testimony* **witness**, *tables* **slabs** of stone,
*written* **inscribed** with the finger of *God* **Elohim**.

## THE SHABBATH IN THE NEW COVENANT: THE FORESHABBATH

- {4315} **prosabbaton** *noun* pre—shabbath

## YAH SHUA ENTOMBED

**Only in Markos 15:42, 43**

And *now when the even was come*
**already being evening**,
because it was the preparation,
that is, the *day before the sabbath* **foreshabbath** {4315},
*Joseph* **Yoseph** of *Arimathaea* **Rahmah**,
*an honourable* **a respected** counsellor,
which also *waited for* **awaited**
the *kingdom* **sovereigndom** of *God* **Elohim**,
came, and *went in boldly* **dared go in** unto *Pilate* **Pilatos**,
and *craved* **asked for** the body of *Jesus* **Yah Shua**.

## THE FIRST SHABBATHS

- {3391} **mia** *adjective* first
- {4521} **sabbaton**, **sabbata** *noun* shabbath, shabbaths: often mistranslated, week.

The First Shabbath may correspond to the Foreshabbath of Markos 15:42.

**Yah Chanan 20:1**

**On** the **first** *day* of the *week* **shabbaths** {4521}
cometh *Mary* **Miryam the** Magdalene
**in the** early **morning**, when it was yet dark,
unto the *sepulchre* **tomb**,
and seeth the stone taken away from the *sepulchre* **tomb**.

## THE RESURRECTED YAH SHUA APPEARS TO TEN DISCIPLES

**Yah Chanan 20:19**

*Then* **So** the same day at evening,
being the **first** *day of the week* **shabbaths** {4521},
when the *doors* **portals** were shut
where the disciples were assembled
for *fear* **awe** of the *Jews* **Yah Hudiym**,
came *Jesus* **Yah Shua** and stood in the midst,
and *saith* **wordeth** unto them,
*Peace* **Shalom** *be* unto you.

**Matthaios 28:1**
In the *end* **eve** of the *sabbath* **shabbaths**,
as it began to dawn
*toward* **unto** the **first** *day of the week* **shabbaths**,
came *Mary* **Miryam the** Magdalene
and the other *Mary* **Miryam**
to *see* **observe** the *sepulchre* **tomb**.

**Markos 16:1,2**
And when the *sabbath* **shabbath** was past,
*Mary* **Miryam the** Magdalene,
and *Mary* **Miryam** the mother of *James* **Yaaqovos**,
and *Salome* **Shalome**,
had bought *sweet spices* **aromatics**,
that they might come and anoint him.
And very early in the morning
the **first** *day* of the *week* **shabbaths**,
they came unto the *sepulchre* **tomb**
at the rising of the sun.

## YAH SHUA, ADONAY OF THE SHABBATH

**Loukas 6:1—3**
And **so be** it *came to pass*
on the second *sabbath after the first* **first shabbath**,
that he went through the *corn fields* **spores**;
and his disciples plucked the *ears of corn* **kernels**,
and did eat, rubbing them in their hands.
And *certain* **some** of the Pharisees said unto them,
Why do ye that which is not *lawful* **allowed** to do
on the *sabbath days* **shabbaths**?
And *Jesus* **Yah Shua** answering them said,
Have ye not read so much as this, what David did,
when himself *was an hungred* **famished**,
and they which were with him;
How he *went* **entered** into the house of *God* **Elohim**,
and did take and eat the *shewbread* **prothesis bread**,
and gave also to them that were with him;
which it is not *lawful* **allowed** to eat
*but* **except** for the priests alone?

**Acts 20:7**
And upon the **first** *day of the week* **shabbath**,
when the disciples *came* **assembled** together
to break bread,
*Paul preached* **Paulos reasoned** unto them,
*ready* **about** to depart on the morrow;
and *continued* **stretched** his *speech* **words**
until midnight.

## CONTRIBUTIONS

**1 Corinthians 16:1,2**
Now concerning the *collection* **contribution**
*for* **to** the *saints* **holy**,
**exactly** as I have *given order* **ordained**
to the *churches* **ecclesiae** of Galatia, even *so* **thus** do ye.
Upon the **first** *day* of the *week* **shabbath**
let *every one* **each** of you *lay* **place** by him *in store*,
*as God hath* **treasuring up as ever he** prospered *him*,
that there be no *gatherings* **contributions** when I come.

## YAH SHUA, ADONAY OF THE SHABBATH

**Matthaios 12:1—14**

At that *time* **season**
*Jesus* **Yah Shua** went on the *sabbath day* **shabbath**
through the *corn* **spores**;
and his disciples were *an hungred* **famished**,
and began to pluck the *ears of corn* **cobs** and to eat.
But when the Pharisees saw it, they said unto him,
Behold,
thy disciples do that which is not *lawful* **allowed** to do
*upon the sabbath day* **in shabbath**.
But he said unto them,
Have ye not read what David did,
when he was *an hungred* **famished**,
and they that were with him;
How he entered into the house of *God* **Elohim**,
and did eat the *shewbread* **prothesis bread**,
which was not *lawful* **allowed** for him to eat,
neither for them which were with him,
*but* **except** only for the priests?
Or have ye not read in the *law* **torah**,
how that on the *sabbath days* **shabbaths**
the priests in the *temple* **priestal precinct**
profane the *sabbath* **shabbath**,
and are *blameless* **unaccused**?
But I *say* **word** unto you,
That *in this place is one greater than the temple*
**a greater than the priestal precinct is here.**

But if ye had known what this *meaneth* **be**,
I will *have* mercy, and not sacrifice,
ye *would* **should** not
have *condemned* **adjudged** the *guiltless* **unaccused**.
For the Son of *man* **humanity** is *Lord* **Adonay**
even of the *sabbath day* **shabbath**.

## YAH SHUA HEALS ON THE SHABBATH

And when he was departed thence,
he went into their synagogue:
And, behold,
there was a *man* **human** which had his hand withered.
And they asked him, *saying* **wording**,
Is it *lawful* **allowed**
to *heal* **cure** on the *sabbath days* **shabbaths**?
that they might accuse him.
And he said unto them,
What *man* **human** shall there be *among* **of** you,
that shall have one sheep,
and *if* **whenever** it fall into a *pit* **cistern**
on the *sabbath day* **shabbaths**,
*will* **shall** he not *lay hold on* **indeed, overpower** it,
and lift it out?
**So** How much *then*
*is a man better than* **a human surpasseth** a sheep?
*Wherefore* **So** it is *lawful* **allowable** to do well
on the *sabbath days* **shabbaths**.

Then *saith* **wordeth** he to the *man* **human**,
*Stretch forth* **Extend** thine hand.
And he *stretched* **extended** it *forth*;
and it was restored whole, like as the other.
*Then* **And** the Pharisees went out,
and *held a* **took** council against him,
how they might destroy him.

## AND NOW, JUMPING TO CONCLUSIONS

**Markos 2:27, 28**

And he *said* **worded** unto them,
The *sabbath* **shabbaths**
*was made* **became** for *man* **humanity**,
and not *man* **humanity** for the *sabbath* **shabbaths**:
*Therefore* **So then** the Son of *man* **humanity**
is *Lord* **Adonay** also of the *sabbath* **shabbath**.

In your opinion,
Does this verse give you an escape from guarding the Shabbath?

________________________________________

________________________________________

________________________________________

## AND NOW, FOR MY SECOND JUMP TO CONCLUSIONS

**Colossians 2:16, 17**

Let no *man* **one** therefore judge you
in *meat* **food**, or in drink,
or in *respect of an holyday* **apportioning a celebration**,
or of the new moon, or of the *sabbath days* **shabbaths**:
Which are a shadow of *things to come* **the about to be**;
but the body is of *Christ* **ha Mashiyach**.

**Big Question**

Do the verses above allow you to eat and drink whatever and as much as you desire — or to guard or break the Shabbath?

________________________________________

________________________________________

________________________________________

# 145 Apocalypses of

## APOCALYPSE

- {601} **apokalupto** *verb* unveiling
- {602} **apokalupsis** *noun* unveiling

Here we are at the final segment of our journey. Up til now we have presented PANORAMAS — overviews of Scripture subjects, VIGNETTES — snapshots of shorter themes; and now we are approaching the APOCALYPSES — the unveilings of precious treasures all with one ultimate goal — of encouraging you — yea, challenging you to not only enter the holy of holies, but to abide in the holy of holies — the very presence of the Creator and the saviour, in the radiance of his Shechinah Glory.

## RETROSPECTUS:

### Where I've been

Describe concisely, your spiritual journey up to the time you began reading this book:

________________________________________

________________________________________

________________________________________

________________________________________

________________________________________

# Retrospect 146

## INTROSPECTUS:
### Where I am now

Describe concisely, your spiritual journey since you began reading this book:

________________________________________

________________________________________

________________________________________

The DATE is: __________________________

The TIME is: __________________________

The rest of my life begins ____________________.

## PROSPECTUS:
### Where I will to journey

Dear Creator of the universe, and saviour of all humanity, I hereby will to offer you my body, soul, and spirit, to ever abide in your presence.

Open now heart and mind with knowledge, wisdom, and discernment — to grasp every nugget of truth that you have treasured for me.

________________________________________

________________________________________

________________________________________

________________________________________

____________________________

signed

Amen.

# 147 Apocalypses of

## APOCALYPSE OF ABIDING IN ABODES

• {3306} **meno** *verb* to abide:

**The Holy Spirit Abode In Yah Shua**

**Yah Chanan 1:32—34**
And *John bare record* **Yahn witnessed**,
*saying* **wording**,
I saw the Spirit descending from *heaven* **the heavens**
*like* **as** a dove,
and it abode {3306} upon him.
And I knew him not:
but he that sent me to baptize *with* **in** water,
the same said unto me,
Upon whom **ever** thou shalt see the Spirit descending,
and *remaining* **abiding** {3306} on him,
the same is he
which baptizeth *with* **in** the Holy *Ghost* **Spirit**.
And I saw, and *bare record* **witnessed**
that this is the Son of *God* **Elohim**.

## THE RHEMA OF YAH VEH ABIDES UNTO THE EONS

**1 Petros 1:25**
But the *word* **rhema** of *the Lord* **Yah Veh**
*endureth for ever* **abideth** {3306} **unto the eons**.
And this is the *word* **rhema**
*which by the gospel is preached* **evangelized** unto you.

## CO—ABIDING SHALAMS HIS LOVE IN US

**1 Yah Chanan 4:12—16**
No *man* **one** hath *seen God* **observed Elohim**
*at any time* — **not ever**.
*If* **Whenever** we love one another,
*God dwelleth* **Elohim abideth** {3306} in us,
and his love is *perfected* **completed/shalamed** in us.
*Hereby* **In this** know we
that we *dwell* {3306} **abide** in him, and he in us,
because he hath given us of his Spirit.
And we have *seen* **observed** and *do testify* **witness**
that the Father *sent* **apostolized** the Son
*to be the* Saviour of the *world* **cosmos**.
Whosoever shall *confess* **profess**
that *Jesus* **Yah Shua** is the Son of *God* **Elohim**,
*God dwelleth* **Elohim abideth** {3306} in him,
and he in *God* **Elohim**.
And we have known and *believed* **trusted** the love
that *God* **Elohim** hath *to* **in** us.
*God* **Elohim** is love;
and he that *dwelleth* {3306} **abideth** in love
*dwelleth* {3306} **abideth** in *God* **Elohim**,
and *God* **Elohim** in him.

**1 Corinthians 13:13**
And now abideth {3606} *faith* **trust**, hope, *charity* **love**,
these three;
but the greatest of these is *charity* **love**.

# Abide, Abode 148

## CO—ABIDING IN THE VINE

**Yah Chanan 15:1—16**

*I am* **I AM** the true vine,
and my Father is the *husbandman* **cultivator**.
Every branch in me that beareth not fruit
he taketh away:
and every branch that beareth fruit,
he *purgeth* **purifieth** it,
that it may *bring forth* **bear much** more fruit.
*Now* **Already** ye are *clean* **pure** through the word
which I have spoken unto you.
Abide {3306} in me, and I in you
**Exactly** as the branch cannot bear fruit of itself,
*except* **unless** it abide {3306} in the vine;
*no more* **thus neither** can ye,
*except* **unless** ye abide {3306} in me.
*I am* **I AM** the vine, ye are the branches:
He that abideth {3306} in me, and I in him,
the same *bringeth forth* **beareth** much fruit:
for *without* **apart from** me ye can do *nothing* **naught**.
*If a man* **Unless anyone** abide {3306} *not* in me,
he is cast *forth* as a branch, and is withered;
and men gather them,
and cast them into the fire, and they are burned.
*If* **Whenever** ye abide {3306} in me,
and my *words* **rhema** abide in you,
*ye shall* ask what ye will, and it shall be *done* unto you.
Herein is my Father glorified, that ye bear much fruit;
so shall ye be my disciples.

**Exactly** As the Father hath loved me,
so have I loved you:
*continue* {3306} **abide** ye in my love.
*If* **Whenever** ye *keep* **guard** my *commandments* **misvoth**,
ye shall abide {3306} in my love;
even **exactly** as I have *kept* **guarded**
my Father's *commandments* **misvoth**,
and abide {3306} in his love.
These *things* have I spoken unto you,
that my *joy* **cheer** might *remain* **abide** in you,
and that your *joy* **cheer** might be full.
This is my *commandment* **misvah**,
That ye love one another, **exactly** as I have loved you.
Greater love hath no *man* **one** than this,
that *a man lay down* **one place** his *life* **soul** for his friends.
Ye are my friends, *if* **whenever** ye do
*whatsoever* **as much as ever** I *command* **misvah** you.

## THE NEW RELATIONSHIP

Henceforth I *call* **word** you not servants;
for the servant knoweth not what his lord doeth:
but I have *called* **said of** you friends;
for all *things* that I have heard of my Father
I have made known unto you.
Ye have not chosen me, but I have chosen you,
and *ordained* **set** you,
that ye should go and *bring forth* **bear** fruit,
and that your fruit should *remain* **abide** {3306}:
that whatsoever ye shall ask of the Father in my name,
he may give it you.

# 149 Apocalypses of

Abide — how rich the word when the depths of its meaning are experienced.

• {1961} **epimeno** *verb* to abide in

**Romans 6:1,2**

What shall we say then?
shall we *continue* **abide** {1961} in sin,
that *grace* **charism** may *abound* **superabound**?
*God forbid* **So be it not**.
How shall we that are dead to sin,
**still** live *any longer* therein?

**Philippians 1:23—25**

For I am *in a strait betwixt* **overtaken by** two,
having a *desire* **panting** to depart,
and to be with *Christ* **ha Mashiyach**;
which is *far* **rather much** better:
*Nevertheless* **And** to abide {1961} in the flesh
is *more needful* **necessary** for you.
And having this confidence,
I know that I shall abide {3306}
and *continue* **remain** with you all
*for* **unto** your *furtherance* **advancement**
and *joy* **cheer** of *faith* **the trust**;

**Colossians 1:21—23**

And you,
*that were sometime* **being formerly** alienated
and enemies in *your* mind *by wicked* **in evil** works,
yet now hath he **fully** reconciled
In the body of his flesh through death,
to present you holy and *unblameable* **unblemished**
and *unreproveable* **unaccusable** in his sight:
If **indeed** ye *continue* **abide** {1961} in the *faith* **trust**
*grounded* **founded** and *settled* **grounded**,
and *be not moved away* **not transported**
from the hope of the *gospel* **evangelism**,
which ye have heard,
and which was preached *to every creature* **in all creation**
which is under *heaven* **the heavens**;
whereof I *Paul am made* **Paulos became** a minister;

**1 Timo Theos 4:16**

*Take* heed unto thyself, and unto the doctrine;
*continue* **abide** {1961} in them:
for in doing this thou shalt both save thyself,
and them that hear thee.

# Abide, Abode 150

• {2650} **katameno** *verb* abide under

**Acts 1:13, 14**

And when they *were come in* **entered**,
they *went up* **ascended** into an upper *room* **loft**,
where abode {2650} both *Peter* **Petros**,
and *James* **Ya'aqovos**,
and *John* **Yahn** and *Andrew* **Andreas**,
*Philip* **Philippos**, and *Thomas* **Taom**,
*Bartholomew* **Bar Talmay**, and *Matthew* **Matthaios**,
and *James* **Yaaqovos** *the son* of *Alphaeus* **Heleph**,
and *Simon Zelotes* **Shimon the Zealot**,
and *Judas* **Yah Hudah** *the brother* of *James* **Ya'aqovos**.
These all continued *with one accord* **in unanimity**
in prayer and *supplication* **petition**, with the women,
and *Mary* **Miryam** the mother of *Jesus* **Yah Shua**,
and with his brethren.

• {3887} **parameno** *verb* to abide on and on

**1 Corinthians 16:6**

And *it* may *be that* **perhaps**
I *will* **shall** abide {3887} **nearby**,
yea, and winter with you,
that ye may *bring* **forward** me *on my journey*
whithersoever I go.

**Hebrews 7:22—25**

By so much *was Jesus* **hath Yah Shua**
*made a surety* **become a pledge**
of a better *testament* **covenant**.
And they *truly were* **indeed became** many priests,
because they were *not suffered* **forbidden**
to *continue* {3887} **abide** by reason of death:
But this *man* **one**,
because he *continueth ever* **abideth** {3606} **unto the eons**,
hath an *unchangeable* **inviolable** priesthood.
*Wherefore* **So** he is able also
to save them *to the uttermost* **completely**
that come unto *God by* **Elohim through** him,
*seeing he* ever *liveth* **living**
to *make intercession* **intercede** for them.

**Ya'aqovus 1:25**

But whoso looketh
into the *perfect law* **torah of completion/shalom** of liberty,
and *continueth* **abideth** {3887} therein,
he being not a forgetful hearer,
but a doer of the work,
this *man* **one** shall be blessed in his *deed* **doing**.

• {5278} **hupomeno** *verb* to abide under, or through

**Markos 13:13**

And ye shall be hated of all *men* for my name's sake:
but he that shall *endure* **abide** {5278}
unto the *end* **completion/shalom**,
*the* **this** same shall be saved.

# 151 Apocalypses of

**Romans 12:12**
*Rejoicing* **Cheering** in hope;
*patient* **abiding** {5278} in tribulation;
continuing instant in prayer;

**1 Corinthians 13:7**
(Love) *Beareth* **Covereth** all *things*,
*believeth* **trusteth** all *things*,
hopeth all *things*,
*endureth* **abideth** {5278} all *things*.

**2 Timo Theos 2:9—13**
Wherein I *suffer trouble* **endure** {2553} **hardship**,
as an evil *doer* **worker**, *even* unto bonds;
but the word of *God* **Elohim** is not bound.
*Therefore* **So** I endure {5278} all *things*
for the *elect's* **select's** sakes,
that they may also obtain the salvation
which is in *Christ Jesus* **ha Mashiyach Yah Shua**
with eternal glory.
It is a *faithful saying* **trustworthy word**:
For if we *be dead with him* **co—die**,
we shall also *live with him* **co—live**:
If we *suffer* {5278} **abide**,
we shall also *reign with him* **co—reign**:
if we deny *him*, he also *will* **shall** deny us:

## FROM THE CLOUD OF WITNESSES TO YAH SHUA

**Hebrews 12:1—7**
*Wherefore* **So**
seeing we also are *compassed about* **surrounded**
with so *great* **vast** a cloud of witnesses,
let us *lay aside* **put away** every weight,
and the **well—standing** sin *which doth so easily beset us*,
and let us run *with patience* **through endurance**
the *race* **contest** that is set *before* **in front of** us,
*Looking* **Considering** unto *Jesus* **Yah Shua**
the *author* **hierarch** and *finisher* **completer**
of *our faith* **the trust**;
who for the *joy* **cheer** that was set before him
*endured* {5278} **abode** the *cross* **stake**,
*despising* **disesteeming** the shame,
and is *set down at* **seated**
**at** the right *hand* of the throne of *God* **Elohim**.

## THE PURPOSE OF THE DISCIPLINE OF YAH VEH

For consider him
that endured {5278} abode such *contradiction* **controversy**
*of* **by** sinners *against* **unto** himself,
lest ye be wearied and *faint* **weakened**
in your *minds* **souls**.
Ye have not yet *resisted* **withstood** unto blood,
*striving against* **antagonizing with** sin.

# Abide, Abode 152

And ye *have forgotten* **are utterly oblivious**
**to** the *exhortation* **consolation**
which *speaketh* **reasoneth** unto you
as unto *children* **sons**,
My son, *despise* **disregard** not thou
the *chastening* **discipline** of *the Lord* **Yah Veh**,
nor *faint* **weaken**
when thou art *rebuked of* **reproved by** him:
For whom *the Lord* **Yah Veh** loveth
he *chasteneth* **disciplineth**,
and scourgeth every son whom he receiveth.
If ye *endure* **abide** {5278} *chastening* **discipline**,
*God dealeth with* **Elohim offereth** you as with sons;
for what son is he
whom the father *chasteneth* **disciplineth** not?

• {4357} **prosmeno** *verb* to abide on

**Acts 11:22, 23**

*Then tidings of* **And word about** these *things*
*came* **was heard** unto the ears of the *church* **ecclesia**
which was in *Jerusalem* **Yeru Shalem**:
and they *sent forth Barnabas* **apostolized Bar Nabi**,
that he should *go as far as* **pass through unto** Antioch.
Who, when he came,
and had seen the *grace* **charism** of *God* **Elohim**,
*was glad* **cheered**, and *exhorted* **besought** them all,
that with *purpose* **prothesis** of heart
they *would cleave unto the Lord*
**should abide** {5278} **in Adonay**.

**1 Timo Theos 5:5**

Now she that is a widow indeed, and *desolate* **alone**,
*trusteth* **hopeth** in *God* **Elohim**,
and *continueth* **abideth** {5278}
in *supplications* **petitions** and prayers
night and day.

~ ~ ~

• {3438} **mone** *noun* an abode

This noun appears twice in Scripture, and in the same chapter.

## YAH SHUA PROMISES HIS PAROUSIA

**Yah Chanan 14:1, 2, 23**

Let not your heart be troubled:
ye *believe* **trust** in *God* **Elohim**, *believe* **trust** also in me.
In my Father's house are many *mansions* **abodes** {3438}:
if *it were* not *so*, I *would* **should** have *told* **said to** you.

*Jesus* **Yah Shua** answered and said unto him,
*If a man* **Whenever anyone** love me,
he *will keep* **shall guard** my words:
and my Father *will* **shall** love him,
and we *will* **shall** come unto him,
and make our abode {3438} with him.

# 153 Apocalypses of

## ABIDING AT HOME vs AWAY FROM HOME

- {1553} **ekdemeo** *verb* away from home
- {1736} **endemeo** *noun* at home:

**2 Cor 5:1—10**

For we know
that *if* **whenever** our earthly house {3614}
of this tabernacle {4636}
*were dissolved* **disintegrated**,
we have *a building* **housing** {3619} of *God* **Elohim**,
an house {3614} not *made with hands* **handmade**,
eternal in the heavens.
For in this we *groan* **sigh**,
*earnestly desiring* **yearning** to be *clothed upon* **endued**
with our house {3613} which is from *heaven* **the heavens**:
If *so be that* **indeed** being *clothed* **endued**
we shall not be found naked.
For we *that are* **being** in this tabernacle {4636}
*do groan* **sigh**,
being burdened:
*not for that we would* **since we will to not**
be *unclothed* **stripped**,
but *clothed upon* **endued**,
that *mortality* **the mortal** might be swallowed *up* of life.
Now he that hath *wrought* **worked** us
for the selfsame *thing* is *God* **Elohim**,
who also hath given unto us
the *earnest* **pledge** of the Spirit.

*Therefore* **So** we are always *confident* **encouraged**,
knowing that, whilst we are at home{1736} in the body,
we are *absent* **away from home** from *the Lord* **Adonay**:
(For we walk *by faith* **through trust**,
not *by sight* **through semblance**:)
We are *confident* **encouraged**, *I say*,
and *willing* **well—approve** rather
to be *absent* **away from home** {1553} from the body,
and to be *present* **at home** {1736} with *the Lord* **Adonay**.
*Wherefore* **So** we *labour* **befriendingly esteem**, that,
whether *present* **at home** {1736},
*or absent* **whether away** {1553} **from home**,
we may be *accepted of* **well—pleasing unto** him.
For we must all *appear* **manifest**
*before the judgment seat* **in front of the bamah**
of *Christ* **ha Mashiyach**;
that *every one* **each** may receive
*the things done in* **through** his body,
*according to* **toward** that he hath *done* **transacted**,
whether *it be* good**,** *or bad* **whether evil**.

## ABIDING IN BODY AND OUT OF BODY

# Abide, Abode 154

## PAULOS IN PARADISE

**2 Corinthians 12:1—7**

It is not beneficial for me to boast:
indeed I come to visions and apocalypses of Adonay.
I knew a human in ha Mashiyach fourteen years ago;
whether in body, I know not;
whether out of the body, I know not:
Elohim knows;
such an one seized to the third heavens.
And I knew such a human,
whether in body, whether out of the body,
I know not; Elohim knows:
that he was seized into paradise
and heard inexpressable rhemas
not allowed for a human to speak.
Of such an one I boast:
yet of myself I boast not — except in my frailties.
For whenever I will to boast, I become not thoughtless;
for I say the truth; but I spare:
lest anyone reckon me above what he sees me,
or somewhat hears of me.

## THE THORN OF PAULOS

And lest I be superciliously exalted
through the excellence of the apocalypses,
I was given a thorn in the flesh
— an angel of Satan to punch me,
lest I be superciliously exalted.

Abide in Me

Abide in me: fast falls the eventide;
The darkness deepens, Lord, with me abide:
When other helpsers fail and comforts flee,
Help of the helpless, O abide in me.

Swift to its close ebbs out life' little day;
Earth's joys grow dim, its glories pass away;
Change and decay in all around I see;
O Thou who changest not, abide in me.

I need thy presence every passing hour;
What but thy grace can fowl the tempter's power;
Who like thyself my guide and stay can be?
Through cloud and sunshine, O abide in me.

Uphold thy stake before my closing eyes;
Shine through the gloom and point me to the skies;
Heaven's morning breaks,
and earth's vain shadow's flee:
In life, in death O Lord, Abide in me.

# 155 Apocalypses of

## HOLY, HOLIES, HALLOWED

- [4720] **miqdash** *noun* holies
- [6918] **qadosh** *noun* holy
- [6942] **qadash** *verb* hallow
- [6944] **qodesh** *noun* holy, holies
- [6944] [6944] **qodesh qodesh** holy of holies
- {37} **hagiazo** *verb* to hallow
- {38} **hagiasmos** *noun* holiness
- {39} **hagion** *noun* holy, holies
- {39} {39} **hagion hagion** *noun* holy of holies
- {40} **hagios** *noun* holy
- {41} **hagiotes** *noun* holiness
- {42} **hagiosune** *noun* holiness
- {48} **hagnizo** *verb* hallow
- {53} **hagnos** *adjective* hallowed
- {3485} **naos** *noun* holy of holies

In your own words, from your own experience, define the following:

holy: ______________________________

hallowed: ______________________________

holy of holies ______________________________

The desire of my heart is that Elohim hallow me, that I be holy.

In my heart I trust that I discern to know its full meaning — but I don't.

Dictionaries describe it away. Theologians say it merely means "set apart". Set apart from what? For what? To what?

Yah Veh says, "Be ye holy, for I am holy." Would you dare say, "Be ye set apart, for I am set apart?"

I don't think so.

It may well be that Elohim has left the full meaning a wee bit unclear, so that we may effort to continually seek and search to fathom the unfathonable — until, in our search, he says, "Well done."

As I am all alone in my 'holy upper room' (yes, I have one), and as I sense his presence over me at this very moment, I have asked him to hallow me with a holiness so that I may impart to you the fervent desire that you may know what it is to be a partaker of his holiness.

To experience the holiness, may I suggest that we all may experience somewhat more intimately what it is to be holy, as we seek to enter his holy presence.

# Holy & Holies 156

**Exodus 3:5**
And he said, *Draw* **Approach** not *nigh* hither:
put off thy shoes from off thy feet,
for the place whereon thou standest
is holy [6944] *ground* **soil**.

**Exodus 13:1, 2**
And *the LORD spake* **Yah Veh worded**
unto *Moses* **Mosheh**, saying,
*Sanctify* **Hallow** [6942] unto me
all the *firstborn* **firstbirthed**,
*whatsoever openeth* **every burster of** the womb
among the *children* **sons** of *Israel* **Yisra El**,
*both of man* **among human** and *of beast* **among animal**:
it is mine.

**Exodus 26:33, 34**
And thou shalt *hang up* **give** the vail
under the *taches* **hooks**,
that thou mayest bring in thither within the vail
the ark of the *testimony* **witness**:
and the vail shall *divide* **separate** unto you
between the *holy place* **holies** [6944]
and **between** the *most holy* **holy** [6944] **of holies** [6944].
And thou shalt *put* **give** the *mercy seat* **kapporeth**
upon the ark of the *testimony* **witness**
in the *most holy place* **holy** [6944] **of holies** [6944].

**Exodus 29:37**
Seven days thou shalt *make an atonement* **kapar/atone**
for the **sacrifice** altar, and *sanctify* **hallow** [6942] it;
and it shall be *an* **a sacrifice** altar
*most holy* — **a holy** [6944] **of holies** [6944]:
whatsoever toucheth the **sacrifice** altar
shall be *holy* **hallowed** [6942].

**Exodus 29:43**
And there I *will meet* **shall congregate**
with the *children* **sons** of *Israel* **Yisra El**,
*and the tabernacle shall be sanctified*
**to be hallowed** [6942] by my *glory*.

**Exodus 30:10**
And *Aaron* **Aharon**
shall *make an atonement* **kapar/atone**
upon the horns of it once in a year
with the blood
of the *sin offering of atonements* **kippurim for sin**:
once in the year
shall he *make atonement* **kapar/atone** upon it
throughout your generations:
it is *most holy* **a holy** [6944] **of holies** [6944]
unto *the LORD* **Yah Veh**.

**Exodus 30:29, 30**
And thou shalt *sanctify* **hallow** [6942] them,
that they may be *most holy* **a holy** [6944] **of holies** [6944]:
whatsoever toucheth them shall be *holy* **hallowed** [6942].
And thou shalt anoint *Aaron* **Aharon** and his sons,
and *consecrate* **hallow** [6942] them, that they may
*minister unto me in the priest's office*
**priest the priesthood unto me**.

**Exodus 31:13, 14**
And Yah Veh words to Mosheh, saying,
Word also to the sons of Yisra El, saying,
Only, guard my shabbaths:
for it is a sign between me and between you
throughout your generations;
that you know I — Yah Veh hallow [6942] you:
guard the shabbath; for it *is* holy [6944] to you:
everyone who profanes it,
in deathifiying, be deathified:
for whoever works any work therein,
that soul becomes cut off from among his people.

**Leviticus 10:3, 4**
Then *Moses* **Mosheh** said unto *Aaron* **Aharon**,
This is it that *the LORD spake* **Yah Veh worded**, saying,
I *will* **shall** be *sanctified* **hallowed** [6942] in them
that come nigh me,
and *before* **at the face of** all the people
I *will* **shall** be *glorified* **honoured**.
And *Aaron held his peace* **Aharon hushed**.
And *Moses* **Mosheh**
called *Mishael* **Misha El** and *Elzapha* **El Saphan**,
the sons of *Uzziel* **Uzzi El** the uncle of *Aaron* **Aharon**,
and said unto them, Come near,
*carry* **bear** your brethren
from *before* **the face of** the *sanctuary* **holies** [6944]
*out of* **without** the camp.

**Leviticus 11:44, 45**
For *I am the LORD* **I — Yah Veh** your *God* **Elohim**:
ye shall *therefore sanctify* **hallow** [6942] yourselves,
and ye shall be holy [6918]; for *I am* **I** — holy [6918]:
neither shall ye *defile yourselves* **foul your souls**
with any *manner of creeping thing* **teemer**
that creepeth upon the earth.
For *I am the LORD* **I — Yah Veh**
that *bringeth* **ascendeth** you *up*
out of the land of *Egypt* **Misrayim**,
to be your *God* **Elohim**:
ye shall therefore be holy [6918], for *I am* **I** — holy [6918]:

**Leviticus 14:13**
And he shall *slay* **slaughter** the lamb
in the place where he shall *kill* **slaughter**
*the sin offering* **that for the sin**
and the *burnt offering* **holocaust**,
in the *holy place* **holies** [6944]:
for as *the sin offering* **that for the sin** is the priest's,
so is *the trespass offering* **that for the guilt**:
it is *most holy* **a holy** [6944] **of holies** [6944]:

**Leviticus 16:33**
And he shall *make an atonement* **kapar/atone**
for the *holy sanctuary* **holy** [6944] **of holies** [4720],
and he shall *make an atonement* **kapar/atone**
for the *tabernacle* **tent** of the congregation,
and for the **sacrifice** altar,
and he shall
*make an atonement* **kapar/atone** for the priests,
and for all the people of the congregation.

# Holy & Holies 158

**Leviticus 19:2**

*Speak* **Word** unto all the *congregation* **witness**
of the *children* **sons** of *Israel* **Yisra El**,
and say unto them, Ye shall be holy [6918]:
for I *the LORD* **Yah Veh** your *God* **Elohim** am holy [6918].

**Leviticus 20:7**

*Sanctify* **Hallow** [6942] yourselves therefore, and be ye holy:
for *I am the LORD* **I — Yah Veh** your *God* **Elohim**.

**Leviticus 20:26**

And ye shall be holy [6918] unto me:
for I *the LORD* **Yah Veh** am holy [6918],
and have *severed* **separated** you from *other* people,
that ye should be mine.

**Psalm 68:5—7**

And the heavens
shall *praise* **extend hands unto** thy *wonders* **marvels**,
O *LORD* **Yah Veh**:
thy *faithfullness* **trustworthiness** also
in the congregation of the *saints* **holy** [6918].
For who in the *heaven* **vapours**
*can* **shall** be *compared* **ranked**
*unto the LORD* **with Yah Veh**?
who among the sons of *the mighty* **El**
*can* **shall** be likened unto *the LORD* **Yah Veh**?
*God* **El** is greatly to be *feared* **awed**
in the *assembly* **private counsel** of the *saints* **holy** [6918],
and *to be had in reverence* **awed**
*of* **over** all them that are about him.

## THE VISION OF YESHA YAH

**Yesha Yah 6:1—3**

In the year that *king Uzziah* **sovereign Uzzi Yah** died
I saw also *the Lord* **Adonay** sitting upon a throne,
high and lifted up,
and his *train* **drape** filled the *temple* **manse**.
Above it stood the *seraphims* **seraphim**:
*each one had* six wings — **six wings to one**;
with *twain* **two** he covered his face,
and with *twain* **two** he covered his feet,
and with *twain* **two** he *did fly* **flew**.
And one *cried* **called** unto another, and said,
Holy [6918], holy[6918], holy[6918],
*is the LORD of hosts* **Yah Veh Sabaoth**:
the whole earth is full of his glory.

**Yah Chanan 1:33**

And I knew him not:
but he that sent me to baptize *with* **in** water,
the same said unto me,
Upon whom **ever** thou shalt see the Spirit descending,
and *remaining* **abiding** on him,
the same is he
which baptizeth *with* **in** the Holy {40} *Ghost* **Spirit**.

# 159 Apocalypses of

**Yah Chanan 17:17—19**
*Sanctify* **Hallow** {37} them *through* **in** thy truth:
thy word is truth.
**Exactly** As thou hast *sent* **apostolized** me
into the *world* **cosmos**,
even so have I also sent them into the *world* **cosmos**.
And for their sakes I *sanctify* **hallow** {37} myself,
that they also might be *sanctified* **hallowed** {37}
*through* **in** the truth.

**Markos 1:4—8**
**And so be it,** *John* **Yahn** did baptize in the wilderness,
and *preach* **preaching** the baptism of repentance
for the *remission* **forgiveness** of sins.
And there *went out* **proceeded** unto him
all the *land* **region** of *Judaea* **Yah Hudah**,
and *they of Jerusalem* **the Yeru Shalemiym**,
and were all baptized of him
in the *river* **stream** of *Jordan* **Yarden**,
*confessing* **homologizing** their sins.
And *John* **Yahn** was *clothed* **endued** with camel's hair,
and with a girdle of *a skin* **leather** about his loins;
and he did eat locusts and wild honey;
And preached, *saying* **wording**,
There cometh one mightier than I after me,
the *latchet* **thongs** of whose shoes
I am not worthy to stoop down and *unloose* **release**.
I indeed have baptized you *with* **in** water:
but he shall baptize you *with* **in** the Holy {40} *Ghost* **Spirit**.

**Markos 1:24**
*saying* **wording**, *Let us alone* **Aha!**;
what have we to do with thee,
thou *Jesus of Nazareth* **Yah Shua the Nazir**?
art thou come to destroy us?
I know thee who thou art,
the Holy {40} One of *God* **Elohim**.

**Lukas 11:2**
And he said unto them,
when **ever** ye pray, *say* **word**,
Our Father which art in *heaven* **the heavens**,
Hallowed {37} be thy name.
Thy *kingdom* **sovereigndom** come.
Thy will *be done* **become**,
as in *heaven* **the heavens**, so in earth.

**Acts 2:4**
And they were all filled **full**
with the Holy {40} *Ghost* **Spirit**,
and began to speak with other tongues,
**exactly** as the Spirit gave them utterance.

**Acts 3:14, 21**
But ye denied the Holy {40} *One* and the Just,
and *desired* **asked a man** — a murderer
to be granted **charism** unto you;
Whom **indeed** the *heaven* **the heavens** must receive
until the times of *restitution* **restoration** of all *things*,
which *God* **Elohim** hath spoken
*by* **through** the mouth of all his holy {40} prophets
*since* **from** the *world began* **eons**.

**Romans 1:4**
And *declared to be* **decreed** the Son of *God* **Elohim**
*with power* **in dynamis**,
according to the spirit of holiness {42},
by the resurrection from the dead:

**Romans 6:19—23**
I *speak after the manner of men* **word as a human**
because of the *infirmity* **frailty** of your flesh:
for **exactly** as ye have *yielded* **presented** your members
servants to *uncleanness* **impurity**
and to *iniquity* **torah violations**
unto *iniquity* **torah violations**;
even *so* **thus** now *yield* **present** your members
servants to *righteousness* **justness** unto holiness {38}.
For when ye were the servants of sin,
ye were *free* **liberated** from *righteousness* **justness**.
What fruit had ye then
in those *things* whereof ye are now ashamed?
for the *end* **completion/shalom** of those *things* is death.
But now being *made free* **liberated** from sin,
and become *servants* **subservient** to *God* **Elohim**,
ye have your fruit unto holiness {38},
and the *end* **completion/shalom,** *everlasting* **eternal** life.
For the wages of sin is death;
but the *gift* **charisma** of *God* **Elohim** is eternal life
*through Jesus* **in Yah Shua ha Mashiyach** our *Lord* **Adonay**.

**Romans 8:26, 27**
Likewise the Spirit also *helpeth* **co—helpeth**
our *infirmities* **frailties**:
for we know not what *we* should pray for
**according** as we *ought* **must**:
but the Spirit *itself*
*maketh intercession* **intercedeth exceedingly** for us
with *groanings which cannot be uttered* **unutterable sighs**.
And he that searcheth the hearts
knoweth what is the *mind* **thought** of the Spirit,
because he *maketh intercession* **intercedeth**
for the *saints* **holy** {40}
according to the will of *God* **Elohim**.

**1 Corinthians 1:2**
Unto the *church* **ecclesia** of *God* **Elohim**
*which is at* **being in** Corinth,
to them that are *sanctified* **hallowed** {37}
in *Christ Jesus* **ha Mashiyach Yah Shua**,
called *to be saints* **holy** {40},
with all that in every place call upon the name
of *Jesus Christ* **Yah Shua ha Mashiyach** our *Lord* **Adonay**,
both their's and our's:

**1 Corinthians 1:30**
But of him
are ye in *Christ Jesus* **ha Mashiyach Yah Shua**,
who of *God* **Elohim** is *made* **become** unto us
wisdom, and *righteousness* **justness**,
and *sanctification* **holiness** {38}, and redemption:
That, *according* **exactly** as *it is written* **scribed**,
He that *glorieth* **boasteth**,
let him *glory* **boast** in *the Lord* **Yah Veh**.

# 161 Apocalypse

**1 Corinthians 6:1, 2**
Dare any of you,
having a matter *against* **toward** another,
*go to law before* **be judged by** the unjust,
and not **indeed** *before* **by** the *saints* **holy** {40}?
*Do* **Know** ye not *know*
that the *saints* **holy** {40} shall judge the *world* **cosmos**?
and if the *world* **cosmos** shall be judged *by* **in** you,
are ye unworthy to judge the *smallest matters* **lesser**?

**2 Corinthians 7:1**
**So** Having *therefore* these *promises* **pre—evangelisms**,
*dearly* beloved, let us *cleanse* **purify** ourselves
from all *filthiness* **staining** of the flesh and spirit,
*perfecting* **fully completing/shalaming** holiness {42}
in the *fear* **awe** of *God* **Elohim**.

**2 Corinthians 7:11**
For behold this *selfsame thing*,
that ye sorrowed *after a Godly sort* **toward Elohim**,
*what carefulness* **how much diligence**
it *wrought* **worked** in you,
*yea, what clearing of yourselves* **rather, pleading**,
*yea, what* **rather,** indignation,
*yea, what fear* **rather, awe**,
*yea, what vehement desire* **rather, yearning**,
*yea, what* **rather,** zeal,
*yea, what revenge* **rather, vengeance**!
In all *things* **these**
ye have *approved* **commended** yourselves
to be *clear* **hallowed** {53} in this matter.

**Ephesians 1:4**
*According* **Exactly** as he hath *chosen* **selected** us in him
*before* **ere** the foundation of the *world* **cosmos**,
that we should be holy {40} and *without blame* **unblemished**
*before him* **in his sight** in love:

**Philippians 4:8**
Finally, brethren,
*whatsoever things* **as many as** are true,
*whatsoever things* **as many as** are *honest* **venerate**,
*whatsoever things* **as many as** are just,
*whatsoever things* **as many as** are *pure* **hallowed** {53},
*whatsoever things* **as many as** are *lovely* **friendly**,
*whatsoever things* **as many as** are
*of good report* **euphonious**;
if *there be* any virtue, and if *there be* any *praise* **halal**,
*think on* **reckon** these *things*.

**1 Thessalonians 3:13**
To *the end he may* stablish your hearts
*unblameable* **unaccusable** in holiness {42}
*before God* **in front of Elohim**, even our Father,
at the *coming* **parousia**
of our *Lord Jesus Christ* **Adonay Yah Shua ha Mashiyach**
with all his *saints* **holy** {40}.

## HOLINESS OVER IMMORALITY

**1 Thessalonians 4:1—7**
*Furthermore then* **So finally** we beseech you, brethren,
and *exhort* **beseech**
you *by the Lord Jesus* **in Adonay Yah Shua**,
that **exactly** as ye have *received* **taken** of us
how ye *ought to* **must** walk and to please *God* **Elohim**,
*so* **that** ye *would abound* **should superabound**
more and more.
For ye know
what *commandments* **evangelisms** we gave you
*by the Lord Jesus* **through Adonay Yah Shua**.
For this is the will of *God* **Elohim**,
even your *sanctification* **holiness** {38},
that ye should abstain from *fornication* **whoredom**:
That *every* **each** one of you should know
how to *possess* **acquire** his vessel
in *sanctification* **holiness** {38} and honour;
Not in the *lust* **passion** of *concupiscence* **panting**,
*even* **exactly** as the *Gentiles* **goyim**
which know not *God* **Elohim**:
That no *man go beyond* **one overstep**
and defraud his brother in any matter:
because that *the Lord* **Adonay**
is the avenger *of* **concerning** all such,
**exactly** as we also have *forewarned* **foretold** you
and *testified* **witnessed**.
For *God* **Elohim** hath not called us
unto *uncleanness* **impurity**, but *unto* **in** holiness {38}.

**2 Thessalonians 2:13**
But we are *bound* **indebted** to *give thanks* **eucharistize**
alway to *God* **Elohim** for you,
brethren beloved of *the Lord* **Adonay**,
because *God* **Elohim** hath from the beginning
*chosen* **selected** you to salvation
*through sanctification* **in holiness** of the Spirit
and *belief* **trust** of the truth:

**Hebrews 8:1, 2**
Now of *the things* **those**
which we have *spoken* **worded,** this is the sum:
We have such an *high* **arch** priest
who is *set* **seated** on the right *hand* of the throne
of the Majesty in the heavens;
A *minister* **liturgist** of the *sanctuary* **Holies** {39},
and of the true tabernacle,
which *the Lord pitched* **Yah Veh staked**,
and not *man* **humanity**.

## THE COSMIC HOLY TABERNACLE

**Hebrews 9:1, 2**
*Then verily* **But indeed** the first *covenant* **tabernacle**
had also
*ordinances* **judgments** of *divine service* **ministration**,
and a *worldly sanctuary* **cosmic Holies** {39}.
For there was a tabernacle *made* **prepared**;
the first, wherein was the *candlestick* **menorah**,
and the table, and the *shewbread* **prothesis bread**;
which is *called* **worded** the *sanctuary* **Holies** {39}.

# 163 Apocalypse

**Hebrews 9:3**
And after the second veil, the tabernacle
which is *called* **worded**
the *Holiest of all* **Holy** {39} **of Holies** {39};

**Hebrews 9:8**
The Holy {40} *Ghost* **Spirit** this *signifying* **evidencing**,
that the way into the *holiest of all* **Holies** {39}
was not yet *made* manifest,
while as the first tabernacle was yet standing:

**Hebrews 9:12—14**
Neither *by* **through** the blood of goats and calves,
but *by* **through** his own blood
he entered in once into the *holy place* **Holies** {39},
having *obtained* **found** eternal redemption *for us.*
For if the blood of bulls and of goats,
and the ashes of an heifer sprinkling the *unclean* **profane**,
*sanctifieth* **halloweth** {37} to the purifying of the flesh:
How much more shall the blood of *Christ* **ha Mashiyach**,
who through the eternal Spirit offered himself
*without spot* **unblemished** to *God* **Elohim**,
*purge* **purify** your conscience from dead works
to *serve* **liturgize** the living *God* **Elohim**?

**Hebrews 9:24—26**
For *Christ* **ha Mashiyach** is not entered into the
*holy places made with hands* **handmade Holies** {39},
*which are the figures* **antitypes** of the true;
but into heaven itself,
now to *appear* **manifest**
in the *presence* **face** of *God* **Elohim** for us:
Nor yet that he should offer himself often,
**exactly** as the *high* **arch** priest
entereth into the *holy place* **Holies** {39} every year
*with* **in** blood of others;
*For then* **Otherwise** must he often have suffered
since the foundation of the *world* **cosmos**:
but now once
in the *end* **completion/shalom** of the *world* **eon**
hath he *appeared* **been manifest** to put away sin
*by* **through** the sacrifice of himself.

# of Holy & Holies 164

**Hebrews 10:10, 11, 14**

*By the* **In** which will we are *sanctified* **hallowed** {37}
through the offering
of the body of *Jesus Christ* **Yah Shua ha Mashiyach**
once *for all*.
And every priest **indeed** standeth daily
*ministering* **liturgizing** and offering
*oftentimes* the same sacrifices **often**,
which can never **ever** take away sins:
For by one offering
he hath *perfected for ever* **completed/shalamed in perpetuity**
them that are *sanctified* **hallowed** {37}.

**Hebrews 10:19—22**

**So** having *therefore*, brethren,
boldness to enter into the *holiest* **Holies** {39}
*by* **in** the blood of *Jesus* **Yah Shua**,
By a *new* **freshly slaughtered** and living way,
which he hath *consecrated* **hanukkahed** for us,
through the veil, that is *to say*, his flesh;
And having *an high* **a mega** priest
over the house of *God* **El**;
Let us *draw* **come** near with a true heart
in full *assurance* **bearance** of *faith* **trust**,
having our hearts sprinkled from an evil conscience,
and our bodies *washed* **bathed** with pure water.

# 165 Apocalypse

### Hebrews 10:29

Of how much *sorer* **worse** punishment,
*suppose* **think** ye,
shall he be *thought* **deemed** worthy,
who hath *trodden under foot* **trampled down**
the Son of *God* **Elohim**,
and hath *counted* **deemed** the blood of the covenant,
*wherewith* **wherein** he was *sanctified* **hallowed** {37},
*an unholy thing* **profane**,
and hath *done despite unto* **insulted**
the Spirit of *grace* **charism**?

### Hebrews 12:10

For they *verily* **indeed** for a few days
*chastened us* **disciplined**
after their *own pleasure* **well—thinking**;
but he for *our profit* **benefit**,
that we might *be partakers* **partake** of his holiness {41}.

### Hebrews 12:14

*Follow peace* **Pursue shalom** with all *men*,
and holiness {38},
*without* **apart from** which
no *man* **one** shall see *the Lord* **Adonay**:

### Hebrews 13:11,12

For the bodies of those *beasts* **live beings**,
whose blood is brought into the *sanctuary* **Holies** {39}
*by* **through** the *high* **arch** priest for sin,
are burned without the *camp* **encampment**.
*Wherefore Jesus* **So Yah Shua** also,
that he might *sanctify* **hallow** {37} the people
*with* **through** his own blood, suffered without the gate.

### Ya'aqovos 3:17

But the wisdom that is from above
is first *pure* **indeed hallowed** {53},
then *peaceable* **at shalom**, gentle,
*and easy to be intreated* **agreeable**,
full of mercy and good fruits, *without partiality* **impartial**,
and *without hypocrisy* **unhypocritical**.

### 1 Petros 1:15, 16

But as he which hath called you *is* holy {40},
so be ye holy {40} in all *manner of conversation* **behaviour**;
Because it is *written* **scribed**,
Be ye holy {40}; *for* **because** I am holy {40}.

### 1 Petros 2:5

Ye also, as *lively* **living** stones,
are built *up* a spiritual house, an holy {40} priesthood,
to offer *up* spiritual sacrifices,
*acceptable* **well—received** to *God* **Elohim**
*by Jesus Christ* **through Yah Shua ha Mashiyach**.

**1 Petros 2:0**

But ye are a *chosen generation* **select genos**,
a *royal* **sovereign** priesthood, an holy {40} *nation* **goyim**,
a peculiar *people* **acquisition unto himself**;
that ye should
*shew forth* **evangelize** the *praises* **exultation** of him
who hath called you out of darkness
into his marvellous light;

**1 Yah Chanan 3:1—3**

*Behold* **Perceive**,
what manner of love
the Father hath *bestowed upon* **given** us,
that we should be called the *sons* **children** of *God* **Elohim**:
*therefore* **because of this** the *world* **cosmos** knoweth us not,
because it knew him not.
Beloved, now are we the *sons* **children** of *God* **Elohim**,
and it *doth* **be** not yet *appear* **manifest**
what we shall be;
but we know that,
*when* **whenever** he shall *appear* **be manifest**,
we shall be like him;
*for* **because** we shall see him **exactly** as he is.
And every *man* **one** that hath this hope in him
*purifieth* **halloweth** {48} himself,
*even* **exactly** as he is *pure* **hallowed** {53}.

**Apocalypse 4:8**

And the four *beasts had* **live beings were**
each *of them* **surrounded with** six wings *about him*;
and *they were* full of eyes within:
and they **have no** rest *not* day and night,
*saying* **wording**, Holy {40}, holy {40}, holy {40},
*Lord God Almighty* **Yah Veh El Sabaoth**,
*which was, and is, and is to come*
**who was, and who is, and who is coming**.

**Apocalypse 22:11**

He that *is unjust* **injureth**,
let him *be unjust* **injure** still:
and he which *is filthy* **fouleth**,
let him *be filthy* **foul** still:
and he that is *righteous* **just**,
let him *be righteous* **justify** still:
and he that is holy {40}, let him be *holy* **hallowed** {37} still.

# 167 Apocalypse

## THE HOLY OF HOLIES

• {3485} **naos** *noun* the holy of holies, into which only the high priests were able to enter.

The Authorized King James Version translates **naos** as **shrine** and **temple:** some versions as **nave**. The dictionary describes **nave** as: The central part of a church, extending from the narthex to the chancel and flanked by aisles — and that, most certainly is not meant here.

**Naos** refers the holy of holies in the tabernacle; and Yah Shua applys it to his body as being the holy of holies of Yah Veh. And Paulos places the body of the hallowed as the holy of holies of the Holy Spirit.

## YAH SHUA PROPHECIES HIS DEATH AND RESURRECTION

**Yah Chanan 2:18—22**

*Then* **So** answered the *Jews* **Yah Hudiym**
and said unto him,
What sign shewest thou unto us,
*seeing* that thou doest these *things*?
*Jesus* **Yah Shua** answered and said unto them,
*Destroy* **Release** this *temple* **holy of holies** {3485},
and in three days I *will* **shall** raise it *up*.
*Then* **So** said the *Jews* **Yah Hudiym**,
Forty and six years
was this *temple* **holy of holies** {3485}in building,
and *wilt* **shalt** thou *rear* **raise** it *up* in three days?
But he *spake* **worded**
*of* **concerning** the *temple* **holy of holies** {3485} of his body.
**So** When *therefore* he was risen from the dead,
his disciples remembered
that he had *said* **worded** this unto them;
and they *believed* **trusted** the scripture,
and the word which *Jesus* **Yah Shua** had said.

# of Holy of Holies 168

**Matthaios 27:51— 53**
And, behold,
the veil of the *temple* **holy of holies** {3485}
was *rent* **split** in twain
from *the top to the bottom* **above to downward**;
and the earth *did quake* **quaked**, and the rocks *rent* **split**;
And the *graves* **tombs** *were* opened;
and many bodies of the *saints* **holy** which slept arose,
And came out of the *graves* **tombs**
after his *resurrection* **rising**,
and *went* **entered** into the holy city,
and *appeared* **manifested** unto many.

**1 Petros 3:19**
and preaching to the souls
being held in sheol.
Aramaic New Covenant

**Markos 15:29, 30**
And they that passed by *railed on* **blasphemed** him,
wagging their heads, and *saying* **wording**, *Ah* **Aha**,
thou that *destroyest* **disintegratest**
the *temple* **holy of holies** {3485},
and buildest it in three days,
Save thyself, and come down from the *cross* **stake**.

## REACTIONS: MATERIAL AND PHYSICAL

**Markos 15:38, 39**
And the veil of the *temple* **holy of holies** {3485}
was *rent* **split** in twain
from *the top* **above** to *the bottom* **below**.
And when the centurion,
which *stood over against* **was present opposite** him,
saw that he *so* **thus** cried out,
and *gave up the ghost* **expired**, he said,
Truly this *man* **human** was the Son of *God* **Elohim**.

**Loukas 1:21, 22**
And the people
*waited for Zacharias* **awaited Zechar Yah**,
and marvelled that he *tarried so long* **took his time**
in the *temple* **holy of holies** {3485}.
And when he came out, he could not speak unto them:
and they *perceived* **knew**
that he had seen a vision
in the *temple* **holy of holies** {3485}:
for he *beckoned* **nodded** unto them,
and *remained speechless* **continually abode mute**.

# 169 Apocalypse

**1 Corinthians 3:16, 20**
Know ye not
that ye are the *temple* **holy of holies** {3485} of *God* **Elohim**,
and that the Spirit of *God* **Elohim** dwelleth in you?
If any *man defile* **one corrupts**
the *temple* **holy of holies** {3485} of *God* **Elohim**,
him shall *God* **Elohim** destroy;
for the *temple* **holy of holies** {3485} of *God* **Elohim** is holy,
which *temple* ye are.
Let no *man deceive* **one seduce** himself.
If any *man* **one** among you
*seemeth* **thinketh** to be wise in this *world* **eon**,
let him become a fool, that he may *be* **become** wise.
For the wisdom of this *world* **cosmos**
is foolishness with *God* **Elohim**.
For it is *written* **scribed**,
He *taketh* **graspeth** the wise
in their own *craftiness* **cunning**.
And again, *The Lord* **Yah Veh** knoweth
the *thoughts* **reasonings** of the wise, that they are vain.

**2 Corinthians 6:16**
And what *agreement* **togetherness**
hath the *temple* **holy of holies** {3485} of *God* **Elohim**
with idols?
for ye are
the *temple* **holy of holies** {3485} of the living *God* **Elohim**;
**exactly** as *God* **Elohim** hath said,
I *will dwell in* **shall indwell** them,
and walk *in* **among** them;
and I *will* **shall** be their *God* **Elohim**,
and they shall be my people.

**Ephesians 2:19—22**
**So** Now *therefore*
ye are no more strangers and *foreigners* **settlers**,
but *fellowcitizens* **co—citizens** with the *saints* **holy**,
and of the household of *God* **Elohim**;
And are built upon the foundation
of the apostles and prophets,
*Jesus Christ* **Yah Shua ha Mashiyach** himself
being the chief corner *stone*;
In whom all the
*building fitly framed together* **co—joined edifice**
groweth unto an *holy temple* **holy of holies** {3485}
in *the Lord* **Adonay**:
In whom ye also are *builded together* **co—settled**
*for an habitation* **unto a settlement** of *God* **Elohim**
*through the* **in** Spirit.

## A PROPHECY OF THE ADVERSARY SEATED IN THE HOLY OF HOLIES

**2 Thessalonians 2:4**
**The adversary,** Who,
*opposeth and exalteth* **superciliously exalting** himself
above all that is *called God* **worded Elohim**,
or that is *worshipped* **venerated**;
so that he, as *God* **Elohim,**
sitteth in the *temple* **holy of holies** {3485} of *God* **Elohim**,
shewing himself that he is *God* **Elohim**.

## THE NEW HOLY HOLY OF HOLIES

**Apocalypse 11:19**
And the *temple* **holy of holies** {3485} of *God* **Elohim**
was opened in *heaven* **the heavens**,
and there was seen in his *temple* **holy of holies** {3485}
the ark of his *testament* **covenant**:
and there *were* **became** lightnings,
and voices, and thunderings,
and *an earthquake* **a quake**, and *great* **mega** hail.

**Apocalypse 15:5—8**
And after *that* **these** I *looked* **perceived**, and, behold,
the *temple* **holy of holies** {3485} of the tabernacle
of the *testimony* **witness** in *heaven* **the heavens** was opened:
And the seven angels
came out of the *temple* **holy of holies** {3485},
having the seven plagues,
*clothed* **endued** in pure and *white* **radiant** linen,
and *having their breasts girded* **girt about the chest**
with golden girdles.
And one of the four *beasts* **live beings**
gave unto the seven angels seven golden *vials* **phials**
full of the *wrath* **fury** of *God* **Elohim**,
who liveth *for ever and ever* **unto the eons of the eons**.
And the *temple* **holy of holies** {3485} was filled with smoke
from the glory of *God* **Elohim**,
and from his *power* **dynamis**;
and no *man* **one** was able to enter
into the *temple* **holy of holies** {3485},
till the seven plagues of the seven angels
were fulfilled/**shalamed**.

**Apocalypse 16:1**
And I heard a *great* **mega** voice
out of the *temple* **holy of holies** {3485}
*saying* **wording** to the seven angels,
Go *your ways*,
and pour out the *vials* **phials**
of the *wrath* **fury** of *God* **Elohim**
*upon* **unto** the earth.

## THE SEVENTH PLAGUE

**Apocalypse 16:17**
And the seventh angel
poured out his *vial* **phial** into the air;
and there came a *great* **mega** voice
out of the *temple* **holy of holies** {3485}
of *heaven* **the heavens**,
from the throne,
*saying* **wording**, It *is done* **hath become**.

## THE OMISSIONS OF THE NEW YERU SHALEM

**Apocalypse 21:22**
And I saw no *temple* **holy of holies** {3485} therein:
for *the Lord God Almighty* **Yah Veh El Sabaoth**
and the Lamb are the *temple* **holy of holies** {3485} of it.

## ENTERING THE HOLY OF HOLIES

How would you like to take a trip? Or, would it sound more desirable if I said, Would you care to embark on a journey with me — to meditate a meditation where few have every ventured — a spiritual life spring of overflowing living waters to refresh your inner spirit — a holy realm where the holy of holies of your total being enters into the very presence of Elohim?

Do you have a beloved with whom you would share this adventurous venture? If you are so graced, read this portion to your beloved, as they meditate. Then have your beloved read to you as you meditate. This will most assuredly reinforce your bond with each other, and most gloriously, reinforce your bond with Elohim himself.

Or, if you are like me, you'll have to go it alone, and effort to read and meditate to yourself.

The results are commensurate with your effort. The more you give, the more you get.

Ready? Turn on your meditator, and go for it.

## THE HOLIES

Visualize with me:

You are sitting in this very building:
and this building is in a wilderness:
— an eleven day journey to the Promised Land
by the direct route:
— forty years when you take the long way:
and visualize this building
completely covered with a tent:

And where you are sitting,
in the Old Covenant, is named,
the Tabernacle of the Congregation.
And in the New Covenant, is named,
The Priestal Precinct.

This is the area where
the Old Covenant Congregation sat:
and where
the New Covenant Ecclesia sat.

This is also the area
where the Apostle Paulos evangelized,
and the area where
Yah Shua ha Mashiyach evangelized.

# of Holy of Holies 172

This is also where the coindealers
and the dovesellers sat —
whose tables our Mashiyach overturned.

It is also known as
THE HOLIES.

Please repeat after me,
THE HOLIES.

~ ~ ~

THE HOLY OF HOLIES
Behind me here,
behind this curtain,
is where the Rabbi Priest entered once a year
to offer for the sins of the people.

In both covenants, it is named,
THE HOLY OF HOLIES.

Please repeat after me,
THE HOLY OF HOLIES.

This is the very place where,
when Elizabeth was bearing Yahn the Baptizer,
her man, Zechar Yah the Rabbi Priest entered,
and seemingly overstayed his time.

When he emerged, he was mute,
and could not speak until he named his son,
Yah Chanan — Friend of Yah.

We have no record of Paul,
or even our Mashiyach,
who is our Rabbi Priest
ever entering the HOLY OF HOLIES.

When our Mashiyach was staked,
the veil of the HOLY OF HOLIES
ripped from above to below
and now all the holy may enter.

Won't you please come in?

# 173 Apocalypse

**Hebrews 9:24—28**

For ha Mashiyach entered not
into a hand—made holies {39},
which are anti—types of the true;
but into the heavens;
to manifest for us at the face of Elohim.
Not that he should offer himself often,
exactly as the arch priest
entering the HOLY {39} OF HOLIES {39}
every year with blood for others;
Otherwise he must have suffered often
since the foundation of the cosmos:
but now, in the completion of the eon,
he manifested to put away sin once[1]
through the sacrifice of himself.
And inasmuch as it is laid out to humanity
to die once[1],
and after this the judgment:
thus ha Mashiyach was offered once[1]
to offer for the sins of many.

**Hebrews 10:10**

*By the* **In** which will we are *sanctified* **hallowed** {37}
through the offering
of the body of *Jesus Christ* **Yah Shua ha Mashiyach**
once[2] *for all*.

once[1] {530} and that is it
once[2] {2178} and that is sufficient

**AND NOW I EVANGELIZE,
The HOLY OF HOLIES
IS NOW OPEN TO YOU.**

**Hebrews 10:19—22**

So having boldness
to enter the HOLY {39} OF HOLIES {39}
by the blood of Yah Shua,
by a new and living way
that he inaugurated for us,
through the veil — that is, his flesh;
having a rabbi priest over the house of Elohim;
let us draw near with a true heart
in full assurance of the trust,
having our hearts sprinkled
from an evil conscience,
and our bodies washed with pure water.

**A WORD**

One evening, in a rather spiritual worship service, many were praying for Yah Shua to enter our worship — and I sensed the Spirit urged me to utter:

I am pleased when you invite me into your presence
which is the HOLIES.

But I invite you into my presence,
which is the HOLY OF HOLIES.

So often, we invite ha Mashiyach into our presence; hopefully that He make a few adjustments to conform to our way of life.

So often, ha Mashiach invites us into his presence, hopefully that we make a few adjustments to conform to His way of life.

Let us unite our spirits in prayer:

I invite you into my presence.

Thank you for entering my presence.

I surrender my total being
— my body of flesh,
my soul,
my spirit.

Allow me to enter the holy of holies of your presence.

Amen.

And now we SING:

I Come into your presence singing,

Halalu Yah; Halalu Yah; Halalu Yah.

HALALU YAH!

# 175 Temples, Tents

## TEMPLES, TENTS, and TABERNACLES

Do you remember, in the Prologue, I mentioned, that as a precious brocade, with golden threads interwoven, you would be transported to a higher level?

Well, that interweaving has already begun in the previous chapter — and from this time forth we shall be defining and redefining, tracing and retracing, iterating and reiterating.

And this is good, for this presents you with knowledge the Scripture — all the Scripture — the Covenants, Old and New are one single entity fitly framed into a single wholeness.

Patience, Dear one — one step at a time. As you move onward, remember where you have been.

In order to prepare us for the Shechinah Glory, there are a few other subjects that would be quite helpful.

It is important for you to master this concise Word Study. You'll experience why as we ever so quickly approach our 'Grand Finale'.

## TEMPLES

The dictionary defines **temple** as a place of religious service.

**Temple**, as we know it, does not appear in Scripture.

### OLD COVENANT:

•[1004] **bayith**, *noun* house; also as a prefix in compound words, as Beth El, House of El.

•[1964] (Hebraic) [1965] (Aramaic) **heykel** *noun* a mansion for sovereigns, as in Shelomoh's manse; the manse of Yah Veh.

### NEW COVENANT:

•{2411} **hieron** *noun* Priestal Precinct; the outer court of the tabernacle where the teaching took place: From {2409} **hierus** *noun* priest.

•{3485} **naus** *noun* the holy of holies of the tabernacle — which we have been and shall be assimilating into our way of life. Won't we?

# 8 Tabernacles 176

## TENTS

- [168] **ohel** *noun* a tent
- [167] **ahal** *verb* to tent.

The **tent** was the abode of the Yisra Eliy. They tented in tents.

**Tent** is also the outer covering of the tabernacle.

Here's a shocker:
The New Covenant has no word for tent.

## TABERNACLES OLD COVENANT:

- [4907] (Aramaic), [4908] (Hebraic) **mishchan** *noun* from [7931] tabernacle; a place of worship.
- [7931] **shachan** *verb* to tabernacle.

## NEW COVENANT:

- {4633} **skene**, {4636} **skenos**, {4638} **skeroma**; *noun* tabernacle;
- {4637} **skenoo** *verb* to tabernacle.
- {4635} **skenopois** *verb* tabernacle makers.
- {4634} **skeenopeegia** *verb* tabernacle peggers.

In the **Old Covenant**, tent and tabernacle are often erroneously and confusingly mistranslated.

How is your memorizer functioning today? If you are able, without too much stress, memorize the first four definitions above.

# 177 Apocalypse of

## APOCALYPSE OF THE METAMORPHOSE

• {3339} **metamorphoo** *verb* to metamorphose: to change into a wholly different form.

• {1096} **ginomai** *verb* to become generated

• [7160] **qeren** *verb* to emit rays: to radiate

These two pages present the **metamorphose** of Yah Shua ha Mashiyach. While Matthaios and Markos explicitly use the word **metamorphose**, Loukas uses the Hellenic **became regenerated**.

As you read these three renderings, ask yourself why Petros suggested making three tabernacles.

## The METAMORPHOSE OF YAH SHUA

**Matthaios 17:1—4**

And after six days *Jesus* **Yah Shua** taketh *Peter* **Petros**,
*James* **Ya'aqovos**, and *John* **Yah Chanan** his brother,
and bringeth them up into an high mountain
*apart* **privately**,
And was *transfigured* **metamorphosed** {3339}
*before* **in front of** them:
and his face *did shine* **radiated** as the sun,
and his *raiment was* **garment became** white as the light.
And, behold, there appeared unto them
*Moses* **Mosheh** and *Elias* **Eli Yah** talking with him.
*Then* **And** answered *Peter* **Petros**,
and said unto *Jesus* **Yah Shua**,
*Lord* **Adonay**, it is good for us to be here:
if thou *wilt* **willest**, let us make here three tabernacles;
one for thee,
and one for *Moses* **Mosheh**, and one for *Elias* **Eli Yah**.

**BIG QUESTION:**

What in the world was Petros thinking, that he even suggest making three tabernacle?

# Metamorphose 178

## THE METAMORPHOSE OF YAH SHUA

**Markos 9:2—6**

And after six days *Jesus* **Yah Shua** taketh with him
*Peter* **Petros**, and *James* **Yaaqovos**, and *John* **Yahn**,
and *leadeth* **bringeth** them *up* into an high mountain
*apart by themselves* **alone**:
and he was *transfigured* **metamorphosed** {3339}
*before* **in front of** them.
And his raiment became *shining* **gleaming**,
*exceeding* **very** white as snow;
so as no fuller on earth can white them.
And there appeared unto them
*Elias* **Eli Yah** with *Moses* **Mosheh**:
and they were talking with *Jesus* **Yah Shua**.
And *Peter* **Petros** answered
and *said* **worded** to *Jesus* **Yah Shua**,
*Master* **Rabbi**, it is good for us to be here:
and let us make three tabernacles;
one for thee, and one for *Moses* **Mosheh**,
and one for *Elias* **Eli Yah**.
For he *wist* **knew** not what to *say* **speak**;
for they were *sore afraid* **utterly frightened**.

**FERVENT QUESTION:**
What in the world was Petros thinking, that he even suggest making three tabernacle?

## THE METAMORPHOSE OF YAH SHUA

**Loukas 9:28—33**:

And **so be** it *came to pass*
about *an* eight days after these *sayings* **words**,
he took *Peter* **Petros** and *John* **Yahn** and *James* **Yaaqovos**,
and *went up* **ascended** into a mountain to pray.
And as he prayed,
the *fashion* **semblance** of his *countenance* **face**
*was altered* {1096} **became regenerated**,
and his *raiment* **garment**
was white and *glistering* **effulgent**.
And, behold, there talked with him two men,
which were *Moses* **Mosheh** and *Elias* **Eli Yah**:
Who appeared in glory,
and *spake* **worded** of his *decease* **exodus**
which he *should accomplish* **was about to fulfill/shalam**
at *Jerusalem* **Yeru Shalem**.
But *Peter* **Petros** and they that were with him
were *heavy* **burdened** with sleep:
and when they were **thoroughly** awake,
they saw his glory, and the two men that stood with him.
And it *came to pass* **became**, as they departed from him,
*Peter* **Petros** said unto *Jesus* **Yah Shua**,
*Master* **Rabbi**, it is good for us to be here:
and let us make three tabernacles;
one for thee,
and one for *Moses* **Mosheh**, and one for *Elias* **Eli Yah**:
not knowing what he *said* **worded**.

**BURNING QUESTION:**
Got it figured out yet?

# 179 Apocalypse of

## THE METAMORPHOSE OF MOSHEH

**Exodus 34:29—35**

And **so be** it *came to pass,*
when *Moses came down* **Mosheh descended**
from mount *Sinai* **Sinay**
with the two *tables* **slabs** of *testimony* **witness**
in *Moses'* **Mosheh's** hand,
when he *came down* **descended** from the mount,
that *Moses wist* **Mosheh knew** not
that the skin of his face *shone* **radiated** [7160]
while he *talked* **worded** with him.
And when *Aaron* **Aharon**
and all the *children* **sons** of *Israel* **Yisra El**
saw *Moses* **Mosheh**, behold,
the skin of his face *shone* **radiated** [7160];
and they *were afraid* **awed** to come nigh him.
And *Moses* **Mosheh** called unto them;
and *Aaron* **Aharon**
and all the *rulers* **hierarchs** of the *congregation* **witness**
returned unto him:
and *Moses talked* **Mosheh worded** with them.

And afterward
all the *children* **sons** of *Israel* **Yisra El** came nigh:
and he *gave* **misvahed** them *in commandment*
all that *the LORD* **Yah Veh** had *spoken* **worded** with him
in mount *Sinai* **Sinay**.
And till *Moses* **Mosheh**
had *done speaking* **finished wording** with them,
he *put* **gave** a vail on his face.
But when *Moses* **Mosheh** went in
*before the LORD* **at the face of Yah Veh**
to *speak* **word** with him,
he *took the* **turned aside his** vail *off,* until he came out.
And he came out,
and *spake* **worded** unto the *children* **sons** of *Israel* **Yisra El**
that which he was *commanded* **misvahed**.
And the *children* **sons** of *Israel* **Yisra El**
saw the face of *Moses* **Mosheh**,
that the skin of *Moses'* **Mosheh's** face *shone* **radiated**:
and *Moses put* **Mosheh returned** the vail
upon his face *again,*
until he went in to *speak* **word** with him.

# Metamorphose 180

**2 Corinthians 3:7, 8**

But if the *ministration* **ministry** of death,
*written and* **inscribings** engraven in stones,
*was glorious* **became in glory**,
so that the *children* **sons** of *Israel* **Yisra El**
could not *stedfastly behold* **stare**
**unto** the face of *Moses* **Mosheh**
for the glory of his *countenance* **face**;
which *glory* was to be *done away* **inactivated**:
How **indeed**
shall not the *ministration* **ministry** of the spirit
be rather *glorious* **in glory**?

**2 Corinthians 3:17, 18**

Now *the Lord* **Adonay** is that Spirit:
and where the Spirit of *the Lord* **Yah Veh** is,
there is liberty.
But we all, with *open* **unveiled** face
*beholding as in a glass* **reflecting**
the glory of *the Lord* **Yah Veh**,
are *changed* **metamorphosed** {3339}
into the same *image* **icon**
from glory to glory,
*even* **exactly** as by the Spirit of *the Lord* **Yah Veh**.

Remember your memory verse?

I am Elohim's creation, I'll live it;
I am Elohim's likeness, I'll look it;
I am Elohim's image, I'll bear it;
I am Elohim's glory, I'll reflect it.

## THE HOLY METAMORPHOSIS

**Romans 12:1, 2**

So I beseech you *therefore*, brethren,
*by* **through** the *mercies* **compassions** of *God* **Elohim**,
that ye present your bodies a living sacrifice,
holy, *acceptable* **well—pleasing** unto *God* **Elohim**,
which is your *reasonable service* **logical liturgy**.
And be not *conformed* **configured** to this *world* **eon**:
but be *ye transformed* **metamorphosed** {3339}
by the renewing of your mind,
that ye may prove what is that good,
and *acceptable* **well—pleasing**,
and *perfect* **completed/shalamed**, will of *God* **Elohim**.

## THE FOUR STAGES OF METAMORPHOSE:

1. conception (gestation}
2. larva (caterpillar)
3. pupa (cocoon}
4. butterfly

You've experienced the gestation; you've crawled around long enough: its time to get out of that cocoon, and fly!

# 181 Apocalypse of

## OH THE GLORY!

- [3519] **kabod** from [3513] *adjective, noun* glorious, glory
- [3513] **kabod** *verb* glorify
- [1935] **howd** *noun* grandeur
- {1391} **doxa** *noun* glory, glorious
- {1392} **doxazo** *verb* glorify
- {1741} **endoxos** *noun* in glory
- {2755} **kenodoxos** *verb* vainly glorifying

**Glory** is about as difficult to define as **holy**. While a number of words are mistranslated **glory**, we shall concern ourselves with those translated accurately. And by presenting these verses, perhaps we may be able to glimpse at the glory of himself, and the glory he bestows upon his beloved.

And as we proceed, we may be lightly treading on verses portraying the **shechinah** and the **shechinah glory**.

## THE GLORY OF YAH VEH

**Exodus 16:7**

And in the morning,
then ye shall see the glory [3519] of *the LORD* **Yah Veh**;
for that he heareth your murmurings
against *the LORD* **Yah Veh**:
and what are we, that ye murmur against us?

**Exodus 16:10**

And **so be** it *came to pass*,
as *Aaron spake* **Aharon worded**
unto the whole *congregation* **witness**
of the *children* **sons** of *Israel* **Yisra El**,
that they *looked* **set their face** toward the wilderness,
and, behold, the glory [3519] of *the LORD* **Yah Veh**
*appeared* **was seen** in the cloud.

**Exodus 24:16, 17**

And the glory [3519] of *the LORD* **Yah Veh**
*abode* **tabernacled** [7931] upon mount *Sinai* **Sinay**,
and the cloud covered it six days:
and the seventh day he called unto *Moses* **Mosheh**
out of the midst of the cloud.
And the *sight* **visage**
of the glory [3519] of *the LORD* **Yah Veh**
was like *devouring* **consuming** fire on the top of the mount
in the eyes of the *children* **sons** of *Israel* **Yisra El**.

**Exodus 33:18—22**
And he said, I beseech thee,
*shew me* **have me see** thy glory [3519].
And he said,
I *will make* **shall cause** all my goodness
pass *before* **in front of** thee,
and I *will proclaim* **shall call**
the name of *the LORD before thee* **Yah Veh at thy face**;
and *will be gracious to* **shall grace**
whom I *will be gracious* **shall grace**,
and *will shew* **shall** mercy *on* whom I *will shew* **shall** mercy.
And he said, Thou canst not see my face:
for there shall no *man* **human** see me, and live.
And *the LORD* **Yah Veh** said, Behold,
there is a place by me,
and thou shalt *stand* **station thyself** upon a rock:
And it shall *come to pass* **become**,
*while* **until** my glory [3519] passeth by,
that I *will* **shall** put thee in a clift of the rock,
and *will* **shall** cover thee with my *hand* **palm**
while I pass by:

## THE GLORY OF YAH VEH FILLS THE TABERNACLE

**Exodus 40:34—36**
Then a cloud covered the tent of the congregation,
and the glory [3519] of *the LORD* **Yah Veh**
filled the tabernacle [4908].
And *Moses* **Mosheh**
was not able to enter into the tent of the congregation,
because the cloud *abode* **tabernacled** [7931] thereon,
and the glory [3519] of *the LORD* **Yah Veh**
filled the tabernacle [4908].
And when the cloud *was taken up* **ascended**
from over the tabernacle,
the *children* **sons** of *Israel* **Yisra El**
*went onward* **pulled stakes** in all their journeys:

**Loukas 2:9**
And, *lo* **behold**, the angel of *the Lord* **Yah Veh**
*came upon* **stood over** them,
and the glory of *the Lord* **Yah Veh**
*shone round about* **haloed** them:
and they *were sore afraid* **awed a mega awe**.

# 183 Apocalypse of

**Loukas 9:30—32**
And, behold, there talked with him two men,
which were *Moses* **Mosheh** and *Elias* **Eli Yah**:
Who appeared in glory,
and *spake* **worded** of his *decease* **exodus**
which he *should accomplish* **was about to fulfill/shalam**
at *Jerusalem* **Yeru Shalem**.
But *Peter* **Petros** and they that were with him
were *heavy* **burdened** with sleep:
and when they were **thoroughly** awake,
they saw his glory, and the two men that stood with him.

## THE WORD BECAME FLESH

**Yah Chanan 1:14**
And the Word *was made* **became** flesh,
and *dwelt* **tabernacled** {4637} among us,
(and we *beheld* **saw** his glory {1391},
the glory {1391} as of
the only *begotten* **birthed** of the Father,)
full of grace and truth.

**Yah Chanan 2:11**
This beginning of *miracles* **signs**
did *Jesus* **Yah Shua** in *Cana* **Qanah** of *Galilee* **Galiyl**,
and manifested *forth* his glory {1391};
and his disciples *believed on* **trusted in** him.

**Yah Chanan 17:5**
And now, O Father,
glorify {1392} thou me with thine own self
with the glory {1391} which I had with thee
*before* **ere** the *world* **cosmos** was.

**Yah Chanan 17:22—24**
And the glory {1391} which thou gavest me
I have given them;
that they may be one, even **exactly** as we are one:
I in them, and thou in me,
that they may be *made perfect* **completed/shalamed** in one;
and that the *world* **cosmos** may know
that thou hast *sent* **apostolized** me,
and hast loved them, as thou hast loved me.
Father, I will that they also, whom thou hast given me,
be with me where I am;
that they may *behold* **see** my glory {1391}.
which thou hast given me:
for thou lovedst me
*before* **ere** the foundation of the *world* **cosmos**.

**1 Corinthians 15:40—44**

*There are* also *celestial* bodies **heavenlies**,
and bodies *terrestrial* **earthly**:
but the glory {1391} of the *celestial* **heavenlies**
is *one* **indeed another,**
and the *glory of the terrestrial* **earthly**
is another.
*There is* one glory {1391} of the sun,
and another glory {1391} of the moon,
and another glory {1391} of the stars:
for *one* star
*differeth from another*
**thoroughly surpasseth** star in glory {1391}.
*So* **Thus** also is the resurrection of the dead.
*It is sown* **spored** in corruption;
*it is* raised in incorruption:
*It is sown* **spored** in dishonour;
*it is* raised in glory {1391}:
*it is sown* **spored** in *weakness* **frailty**;
*it is* raised in *power* **dynamis**:
*It is sown* **spored** a *natural* **soulical** body;
*it is* raised a spiritual body.
There is a *natural* **soulical** body,
and there is a spiritual body.

**2 Corinthians 3:7—11**

But if the *ministration* **ministry** of death,
*written and* **inscribings** engraven in stones,
*was glorious* **became in glory** {1391},
so that the *children* **sons** of *Israel* **Yisra El**
could not *stedfastly behold* **stare**
**unto** the face of *Moses* **Mosheh**
for the glory {1391} of his *countenance* **face**;
which *glory* was to be *done away* **inactivated**:
How **indeed**
shall not the *ministration* **ministry** of the spirit
be rather *glorious* **in glory**?
For if the *ministration* **ministry** of condemnation
*be* glory {1391},
much more *doth*
the *ministration* **ministry** of *righteousness* **justness**
*exceed* **superaboundeth** in glory {1391}.
For even that which was *made glorious* **glorified** {1392}
had no glory {1392} in this *respect* **part**,
*by reason* **because** of the glory that excelleth.
For if that which is *done away* **inactivated**
was *glorious* **through glory** {1391},
much more that which *remaineth* **abideth**
*is glorious* **be in glory** {1391}.

# 185 Apocalypse of

**2 Corinthians 3:18**
But we all, with *open* **unveiled** face
*beholding as in a glass* **reflecting**
the glory {1391} of *the Lord* **Yah Veh**,
are *changed* **metamorphosed** into the same *image* **icon**
from glory {1391} to glory {1391},
*even* **exactly** as by the Spirit of *the Lord* **Yah Veh**.

**Philippians 2:11**
And that every tongue should *confess* **avow**
that *Jesus Christ* **Yah Shua ha Mashiyach** is *Lord* **Adonay**,
to the glory {1391} of *God* **Elohim** the Father.

**1 Petros 5:1**
The elders which are among you I *exhort* **beseech**,
*who am also an elder* — **a co—elder**,
and a witness of the sufferings of *Christ* **ha Mashiyach**,
and also a partaker of the glory {1391}
that shall be *revealed* **unveiled**:

**1 Petros 5:4**
And when the *chief* **Arch** Shepherd
shall *appear* **manifest**,
ye shall receive a *crown* **wreath** of glory {1391}
*that fadeth not away* — **amaranthine**.

**1 Petros 5:10**
But the *God* **Elohim** of all *grace* **charism**,
who hath called us unto his eternal glory {1391}
*by Christ Jesus* **in ha Mashiyach Yah Shua**,
after that ye have suffered a *while* **little**,
*make* **prepare** you *perfect*, stablish,
*strengthen* **invigorate**, *settle* **found** *you*.

## THE NEW YERU SHALEM

**Apocalypse 21:10, 11**
And he *carried* **bore** me away in *the* spirit
to a *great* **mega** and high mountain,
and shewed me that *great city* **megalopolis**,
the holy *Jerusalem* **Yeru Shalem**,
descending out of *heaven* **the heavens** from *God* **Elohim**,
Having the glory {1391} of *God* **Elohim**:
and her light *was* like unto a stone most precious,
*even like* **as** a jasper stone, *clear as crystal* **crystaline**;

**Apocalypse 21:23—26**
And the city had no need of the sun,
neither of the moon, to *shine* **manifest** in it:
for the glory {1391} of *God did lighten* **Elohim lightened** it,
and the Lamb is the *light* **candle** thereof.
And the *nations* **goyim** of them which are saved
shall walk in the light of it:
and the *kings* **sovereigns** of the earth
do bring their glory {1391} and honour into it.
And the gates of it
shall not **no way** be shut *at all* by day:
for there shall be no night there.
And they shall bring the glory {1391} and honour
of the *nations* **goyim** into it.

# 187 Apocalypse of

## APOCALYPSE OF THE SHECHINAH

Have you ever heard someone wax eloquently about the Shechinah Glory? And my heart was always touched by the mystery of it — an unexplored territory to which I had never attained.

Whenever I asked the evangelist of the Scripture, or Strong's Concordance Numbers, they had no answer — until a few months ago.

And in rapid succession I had two confirmations — one, a theologian who preached on the subject, and backed it up with Scripture and Strong's Concordance numbers; and two, a 400 page out of print book more than a century old.

And with those two points of reference, plus my own limited Spirituals of Wisdon, Knowledge, and Discernment, I shall tread slowly but firmly. For it is the utmost prayer of my life that you receive this book — this representation of my life experiences, and that it transport you into the presence of the Shechinah Glory.

**QUESTION**:

What do these names have in common?

Elijah,
Isaiah,
Nehemiah,
Jeremiah,
Shechaniah?

**ANSWER**:

The suffix of each of these names is a mistranslation of the name, Yah. Here is how they are transliterated in all exeGeses Bibles:

Eli Yah,
Yesha Yah,
Yerme Yah,
Nechem Yah,
Zechar Yah,
Shechan Yah.

All that to say this:

The closest that Scripture comes to **shechinah** is the name **Shechan Yah** [7935] which is derived from [7931] shachan *verb* to tabernacle, and [3050] Yah *name* the short form of Yah Veh

In ten verses of Scripture, all that is mentioned about Shechan Yah is his lineage, and a confession of sin. So that does not help us much in our search for the Shechinah Glory, does it?

# the Shechinah 188

Please **examine** these words very carefully:

**OLD COVENANT:**

- [4908] **mishchan** *noun* tabernacle
- [7931] (Hebrew) **shachan** *verb* to tabernacle
- [7932] (Aramaic) **shechan** *verb* to tabernacle
- [7933] **shechen** *noun* tabernacle
- [7934] **shachen** *noun* fellow tabernacler
- [7935] **shechan yah** *name* Tabernacle of Yah
- {4633} **skene** *noun* tabernacle

**NEW COVENANT:**

- {4634} **skenopegia** *noun* tabernacle pegging
- {4635} **skenopoios** *noun* tabernacle maker
- {4636} **skenos** *noun* tabernacle
- {4637} **skenoo** verb tabernacle

**NOTE:** The Hebrew **ch** is sometimes mistranslated **k**. The Hellene has no **ch**, and uses the **k** throughout.

Now let us take our sweet time, and examine the usages of these words in Scripture. Who knows, we may yet attain to the Holy of Holies of the Shechinah Glory. Well, Glory!

Please **analyze** these words very carefully:

• [4908] **mishchan**: The Hebrew alphabet had no vowels until the eighth century. **Mishchan** could just as easily been scribed **mishechen** or **shechen** with a prefix, as [7933] **shechen**.

• [7931] **Shachan** and [7932] **shechan** are *verbs*; and these being the root, **shechinah** must needs be a *verb* — unless it is built on [7933] **shechen** *noun* — which is possible.

The Hellenic has no **V**, no **Y**, no **SH**. Note the similarity to the Hebrew just by changing **s** to **sh**.

Now to the crux of the crisis: How do we get from **tabernacle** to **shechinah**? Good question, you say.

• [7931] **shachen** *verb* is also translated as **abide** and **abode** (past and present tenses).

After all, the **tabernacle** *noun* was the **abode** *noun* of Elohim, wherein he **tabernacled** *verb* **abode** *verb*.

Let us see where this route takes us.

## SHECHINAH

As we begin our journey to explore the mystery of the **shechinah**, we shall hope, not only for understanding, but also for fulfillment in our lives. And for a point of embarkment, we shall examine Scripture and discover how it was bestowed on the trustworthy in Elohim.

In our chapter on Abide, Abode we discussed the deeper meaning of abide. And as we ponder the thought of Yah Veh entering the tabernacle, we realize that it was much more than a place to stay, remain, or dwell. In the context of the message of Yah Shua on the vine and the branches, we begin to grasp that **abide** is to **become a oneness with**.

And as we explore into the depths that the **mishchan** is his **abode**, and **shechin** is his **abiding**, we just begin to fathom the **glory** that is ours as we respond to his invitation to **abide** in the **glory** of his **abode**, and become partakers of his **shechinah glory.**

In our research, we shall present the English **translation** and the Herbaic/Aramaic **transliteration** thus: **tabernacle/shechinah**.

Yah Shua the prophet speaks of the Mishchan that Yah Veh Shechineth

**Yah Shua 22:19 19**

*Notwithstanding* **Surely**,
if the land of your possession be *unclean* **foul**,
*then* pass ye over unto the land
of the possession of *the LORD* **Yah Veh**,
wherein *the LORD'S* **Yah Veh's** tabernacle [4908] **mishchan**
*dwelleth* **tabernacleth** [7031] **shachineth**,
and take possession among us:
but rebel not against *the LORD* **Yah Veh**,
nor rebel against us,
in building you *an* **a sacrifice** altar
*beside* **except** the **sacrifice** altar
of *the LORD* **Yah Veh** our *God* **Elohim**.

## THE GLORY OF YAH VEH FILLS THE HOUSE

**YECHEZQ EL 43:1—9**

Afterward he *brought* **carried** me to the *gate* **portal**,
*even* the *gate* **portal**
that *looketh toward* **faceth the way of** the east:
And, behold,
the glory of *the God* **Elohim** of *Israel* **Yisra El**
came from the way of the east:
and his voice was like a *noise* **voice** of many waters:
and the earth shined with his glory.
And it was according to the *appearance* **vision**
of the vision which I saw,
even according to the vision that I saw
when I came to *destroy* **ruin** the city:
and the visions were like the vision that I saw
by the river *Chebar* **Kebar**;
and I fell upon my face.
And the glory of *the LORD* **Yah Veh**
came into the house by the way of the *gate* **portal**
*whose prospect is toward* **at the face of the way**
**of** the east.
So the spirit *took* **bore** me *up*,
and brought me into the inner court; and, behold,
the glory of *the LORD* **Yah Veh** filled the house.
And I heard him speaking unto me out of the house;
and the man stood *by* **beside** me.

And he said unto me, Son of *man* **humanity**,
the place of my throne,
and the place of the soles of my feet,
where I *will dwell* **shall tabernacle** [7928] **shechan**
in the midst of the *children* **sons** of *Israel* **Yisra El**
*for ever* **eternally**,
and my holy name,
shall the house of *Israel* **Yisra El** no more *defile* **foul**,
neither they, nor their *kings* **sovereigns**,
by their whoredom,
nor by the carcases of their *kings* **sovereigns**
in their *high places* **bamahs**.
In their *setting* **giving** of their threshold
by my thresholds,
and their post *by* **beside** my posts,
and the wall between me and **between** them,
they have even *defiled* **fouled** my holy name
by their *abominations* **abhorrences**
that they have *committed* **worked**:
wherefore I have *consumed* **finished** them **off**
in *mine anger* **my wrath**.
Now let them *put away* **far remove** their whoredom,
and the carcases of their *kings* **sovereigns**,
**remove** far from me,
and I *will dwell* **shall tabernacle** [7931] **shechen**
in the midst of them *for ever* **eternally**.

## THE SHECHINAH IN THE TABERNACLE CLOUD COVER

**Numbers 9:15—23**
And on the day that the tabernacle was *reared up* **raised**
the cloud covered the tabernacle [4908] **mishchan**,
*namely*, the tent [168] of the *testimony* **witness**:
and at even there was upon the tabernacle [4908] **mishchan**
as *it were the appearance* **the visage** of fire,
until the morning.
So it was *alway* **continually**:
the cloud covered it *by day*,
and the *appearance* **visage** of fire by night.
And when the **mouth of the** cloud
*was taken up* **ascended** from the *tabernacle* [168] **tent**,
then after that
the *children* **sons** of *Israel journeyed* **Yisra El pulled stakes**:
and in the place
where the cloud *abode* **tabernacled** [7931] **shechinahed**,
there the *children* **sons** of *Israel* **Yisra El**
*pitched their tents* **encamped**.
At the *commandment* **mouth** of *the LORD* **Yah Veh**
the *children* **sons** of *Israel journeyed* **Yisra El pulled stakes**,
and at the *commandment of the LORD* **mouth of Yah Veh**
they *pitched* **encamped**:
*as long as* **all the days**
the cloud *abode* **tabernacled** [7931] **shechinahed**
upon the tabernacle [4908] **mishchan**
they *rested in their tents* **encamped**.
And when the cloud
*tarried long* **prolonged** upon the tabernacle [4908] **mishchan** many days,
then the *children* **sons** of *Israel* **Yisra El**
*kept* **guarded** the *charge* **guard** of *the LORD* **Yah Veh**,
and *journeyed* **pulled stakes** not.
And so it was, when the cloud
was a *few* **number of** days upon the tabernacle [4908] **mishchan;**
according to
the *commandment* **mouth** of *the LORD* **Yah Veh**
they *abode in their tents* **encamped**,
and according to
the *commandment* **mouth** of *the LORD* **Yah Veh**
they *journeyed* **pulled stakes**.
And so *it was*, when the cloud
*abode* **became** from even unto the morning,
and that the cloud *was taken up* **ascended** in the morning,
then they *journeyed* **pulled stakes**:
whether it was by day or by night
that the cloud *was taken up* **ascended**,
they *journeyed* **pulled stakes**.
*Or whether it were* — two days, or a month, or a year,
that the cloud *tarried* **prolonged** upon the tabernacle [4908] **mishchan**,
*remaining* **tabernacling** [7931] **shechening** thereon,
the *children* **sons** of *Israel* **Yisra El**
*abode in their tents* **encamped**,
and *journeyed* **pulled stakes** not:
but when it *was taken up* **ascended**,
they *journeyed* **pulled stakes**.
At the *commandment* **mouth** of *the LORD* **Yah Veh**
they *rested in the tents* **encamped**,
and at the *commandment* **mouth** of *the LORD* **Yah Veh**
they *journeyed* **pulled stakes**:
they *kept* **guarded** the *charge* **guard** of *the LORD* **Yah Veh**,
at the *commandment* **mouth** of *the LORD* **Yah Veh**
by the hand of *Moses* **Mosheh**.

## WHERE YAH VEH CHOOSES TO TABERNACLE/SHECHINAH HIS NAME

**Deuteronomy 12:11**

Then there shall be a place
which *the LORD* **Yah Veh** your *God* **Elohim** shall choose
to cause his name to *dwell* **tabernacle** there;
thither shall ye bring all that I *command* **misvah** you;
your *burnt offerings* **holocausts**, and your sacrifices,
your tithes,
and the *heave offering* **exaltment** of your hand,
and all your choice vows
which ye vow unto *the LORD* **Yah Veh**:

## THE TORAH ON TITHING

**Deuteronomy 14:22, 23**

**In tithing,**
Thou shalt *truly* tithe all the *increase* **produce** of thy seed,
that the field bringeth forth year by year.
And thou shalt eat *before* **at the face of**
*the LORD* **Yah Veh** thy *God* **Elohim**,
in the place which he shall choose
to *place* **tabernacle** his name there,
the tithe of thy *corn* **crop**,
of thy *wine* **juice**, and of thine oil,
and the firstlings of thy *herds* **oxen** and of thy flocks;
that thou mayest learn to *fear* **awe**
*the LORD* **Yah Veh** thy *God always* **Elohim all days.**

## THE TORAH ON PREPARING THE PASACH

**Deuteronomy 16:1, 2**

*Observe* **Guard** the month of Abib,
and *keep* **work** the *passover* **pasach**
unto *the LORD* **Yah Veh** thy *God* **Elohim**:
for in the month of Abib
*the LORD* **Yah Veh** thy *God* **Elohim**
brought thee forth out of *Egypt* **Misrayim** by night.
Thou shalt therefore sacrifice the *passover* **pasach**
unto *the LORD* **Yah Veh** thy *God* **Elohim**,
of the flock and the *herd* **oxen**,
in the place which *the LORD* **Yah Veh** shall choose
to *place* **tabernacle** his name there.

## THE TORAH ON FIRSTLINGS AND TITHES

**Deuteronomy 26:1, 2**

And it shall be,
when thou art come in unto the land
which *the LORD* **Yah Veh** thy *God* **Elohim**
giveth thee for an inheritance,
and possessest it, and *dwellest* **settlest** therein;
That thou shalt take
of the first of all the fruit of the *earth* **soil**,
which thou shalt bring of thy land
that *the LORD* **Yah Veh** thy *God* **Elohim** giveth thee,
and shalt put it in a basket,
and shalt go unto the place
which *the LORD* **Yah Veh** thy *God* **Elohim**
shall choose to place his name there.

# 193 Apocalypse of

## THE SHECHINAH GLORY

In this final chapter on Apocalypses — of unveilings, allow me to lay myself bare before you. I witness before you and before my holy Elohim, at whose face I must stand and have my tears wiped away, I desire naught more than to live every moment of my life filled full with the Holy Spirit and living in the Shechinah Glory.

Many theologians have wrested Scripture to embellish their message. Where I sensed that the verses fit the **glory**, the **shechinah**, or the two together, the **shechinah glory**, they have been, and are now in included this Grand Finale. And if I have erred, it is on the side of not sqeezing a Scripture to fit.

All that to say this: Even though I may have missed some, these following verses fall under the ministry of the **Shechinah Glory**; and I am blessed beyond measure to present them to you.

I beseech, I pray, I plead that you explore this spiritual opportunity to live your live in the presence of his **Shechinah Glory**. Well, **Glory!**

**Exodus 24:16—18**

And the glory of *the LORD* **Yah Veh**
**tabernacled/shechinad** upon mount *Sinai* **Sinay**,
and the cloud covered it six days:
and the seventh day he called unto *Moses* **Mosheh**
out of the midst of the cloud.
And the *sight* **visage**
of the glory of *the LORD* **Yah Veh**
was like *devouring* **consuming** fire on the top of the mount
in the eyes of the *children* **sons** of *Israel* **Yisra El**.
And *Moses* **Mosheh** went into the midst of the cloud,
and *gat him up* **ascended** into the mount:
and *Moses* **Mosheh** was in the mount
forty days and forty nights.

# Shechinah Glory 194

## SHECHINAH GLORY IN THE NEW COVENANT: REVIEW

- [4908] **mishchan** *noun* tabernacle
- [7931] (Hebrew) **shachan** *verb* to tabernacle
- [7932] (Aramaic) **shechan** *verb* to tabernacle
- [7933] **shechen** *noun* tabernacle
- [7934] **shachen** *noun* fellow tabernacler
- [7935] **shechan yah** *name* Tabernacle of Yah
- {4633} **skene** *noun* tabernacle
- {4636} **skenos** *noun* tabernacle
- {4637} **skenoo** *verb* tabernacle

Remember we said that the Hellenic had no **SH** sound. So vizualize the **S** being **SH**, and the **K** being **CH**, and you'll easily note the relationsip between the Hebraic and the Hellenic.

- {1391} **doxa** *noun* glory
- {1392} **doxazo** *verb* glorify

Now let us begin our search for verses which would indicate the Shechinah Glory in the New Covenant.

## THE WORD BECAME FLESH

**Yah Chanan 1:14**

And the Word *was made* **became** flesh,
and *dwelt* **tabernacled** {4637} **shechinahed** among us,
(and we *beheld* **saw** his glory {1391},
the glory {1391} as
of the only *begotten* **birthed** of the Father,)
full of grace and truth.

**Loukas 2: 9**

And, *lo* **behold**, the angel of *the Lord* **Yah Veh**
*came upon* **stood over** them,
and the glory {1391} of *the Lord* **Yah Veh**
*shone round about* **haloed** {4034} them:
and they *were sore afraid* **awed a mega awe**.

Just as Loukas, being Hellenic, used the words, **became regenerated** instead of **metamorphosed**, he here says the Hellenic **haloed** instead of the Hebraic **shechinahed.**

# 195 Apocalypse of

### The SHECHINAH GLORY HOVERED OVER THE TABERNACLE/MISHECHEM

in the Pillars of Light and Cloud in the wilderness.

### THE SHECHINAH GLORY METAMORPHOSED MOSHE

when his face so radiated that he had to wear a veil to hide his face from the people.

### THE SHECHINAH GLORY TABERNACLED/SHECHINAHED AT THE BIRTH OF YAH SHUA

1. Upon the shepherds **abiding** in the field, when the glory of Yah Veh **haloed/shechinahed** them.

2. And the Word bcame flesh and **tabernacled/shechinahed** among us, and we beheld his **glory**.

### THE SHECHINAH GLORY METAMORPHOSED YAH SHUA IN THE MOUNT

in the presence of Petros, Ya'aqovus, and Yah Chanan.

Now can you see why Petros said, Let us build three tabernacles?

The **tabernacle/mishechen** was the place where Yah Veh **tabernacled/shechinahed/abode**.

# Shechinah Glory 196

## THE SHECHINAH GLORY CAN TABERNACLE OVER US, UPON US, AND WITHIN US

**1 Corinthians 3:16, 17**

Know ye not
that ye are the *temple* **holy of holies** of *God* **Elohim**,
and that the Spirit of *God* **Elohim** dwelleth in you?
If any *man defile* **one corrupts**
the *temple* **holy of holies** of *God* **Elohim**,
him shall *God* **Elohim** destroy;
for the *temple* **holy of holies** of *God* **Elohim** is holy,
which *temple* ye are.

**2 Petros 1:3,4**

According as his divine *power* **dynamis**
hath *given* **graced** unto us all *things*
*that pertain* unto life and *Godliness* **reverence**,
through the knowledge of him
that hath called us *to* **through** glory and virtue:
*Whereby* **Through which** are given unto us
*exceeding great* **magnificent**
and precious *promises* **pre—evangelisms**:
that *by* **through** these
ye might be partakers of the divine nature,
having escaped the corruption
that is in the *world through lust* **cosmos in its pantings**.

## HAVE YOU EVER EXPERIENCED THE HALOED HOLY GLOW OF THE HOLY OF HOLIES TABERNACLING/SHECHINAHING/ ABIDING WITHIN YOU?

Ever meet someone, and within yourself say, "They have such a glow about them?" And possibly they may, or may not, have been one who trusted in ha Mashiyach.

Ever think it possible that you are able to be that one with a holy haloed glow of the shechinah glory over you, upon you, and within you?

That very experience lies before you. It's free, its priceless, and the cost is high — but not prohibitive. It's simply one of the best investments you can make in this lifetime.

I know the shrinks will go after me on this — but it is giving up, surrendering, and submitting. You, alone if need be, must be in one accord and in one place with the Holy Spirit of Elohim.

At least, give it a try — and if, perchance you succeed, think of the smile on the face of Yah Shua as he wipes all tears from all eyes.

You, Dear Friend, can do it. So, do it!

# 197 Grand

# I am Elohim's

# Creation,
# I'll Live it;

______________________
Initial Here

# I am Elohim's

# Likeness,
# I'll Look it;

______________________
Initial Here

# I am Elohim's

# Image,
# I'll Bear it;

Initial Here

# I am Elohim's

# Glory, I'll Reflect it;

Sign Here

## Tell me, What is the difference between soul & spirit?

## Do you know?

There was a time Herb Jahn didn't know either, but felt he needed to know in order to be filled with the Spirit. So he researched the two words. His first discovery? **Soul** was mistranslated into more than forty different words — and **spirit** into more than seven.

After he completed that task, he asked his soul, "What would happen if I researched every word of Scripture?" Little did he realize that at age sixty—five, that was the turning point in his life.

Exegete Herb Jahn then invested seventeen years of his life toward one quest — to discover exactly what every word of Scripture means.

In these seventeen years, Jahn has researched every Word of Scripture — more than 14,000 words — word by word — one word at a time.

Now an octogenarian, Jahn is reaping the reward of his labors, having prepared and published the only Literal Translations & Transliterations of Scripture.

# exeGeses parallel BIBLE

## — two BIBLES, side by side.

• In the left column, the **exeGeses *ready research Bible***, with its myriad exegeses inserted at the points of occurrence, transforms the Authorized King James Version into a Literal Translation & Transliteration.

• In the right column, the **exeGeses *companion Bible***, with the same myriad exegeses in an easy reading, inspirational format.

### exeGeses ready research BIBLE

**LOVE vs BEFRIEND**

**JOHN 21:**

15 So when they had dined,
*Jesus* **Yah Shua**
*saith* **wordeth** to *Simon Peter* **Shimon Petros**,
*Simon* **Shimon**, son of *Jonas* **Yonah**,
Lovest thou me **much** more than these?
He *saith* **wordeth** unto him, Yea *Lord* **Adonay**;
thou knowest that I *love* **befriend** thee.
He *saith* **wordeth** unto him, Feed my lambs.
16 He *saith* **wordeth** to him again the second time
*Simon* **Shimon**, son of *Jonas* **Yonah** Lovest thou me?
He *saith* **wordeth** unto him, Yea *Lord* **Adonay**;
thou knowest that I *love* **befriend** thee.
He *saith* **wordeth** unto him, *Feed* **Shepherd** my sheep.
17 He *saith* **wordeth** unto him the third time,
*Simon* **Shimon**, son of *Jonas* **Yonah**,
*lovest* **befriendest** thou me?
*Peter* **Petros** was *grieved* **sorrowed**
because he *said* **worded** unto him the third time,
*Lovest* **Befriendest** thou me?
And he *said* **worded** unto him, *Lord* **Adonay**,
thou knowest all *things*;
thou knowest that I *love* **befriend** thee.

### exeGeses companion BIBLE

**LOVE vs BEFRIEND**

**YAHN 21:**

15 So they dine,
and Yah Shua
words to Shimon Petros,
Shimon, son of Yonah,
Love you me much more than these?
He words to him, Yes Adonay;
you know I befriend you.
He words to him, Feed my lambs.
16 He words to him again the second time
Shimon, son of Yonah, Love you me?
He words to him, Yes Adonay;
you know I befriend you.
He words to him, Shepherd my sheep.
17 He words to him the third time,
Shimon, son of Yonah,
befriend you me?
Petros sorrows
because he words to him the third time,
Befriend you me?
And he words to him, Adonay,
you know all:
you know I befriend thee.

•Burgundy ISBN 0—9631951—2—3 •Black ISBN 0—9631951—3—1 . . . . .$69.95•

# publishments 206

## The Aramaic New Covenant

**A Literal Translation & Transliteration directly from the language of Yah Shua ha Mashiyach (Jesus Christ). Clarifies many obscure and ambiguous passages.**

Yah Chanan 1:1—4

In the beginning,
the Word having been,
and the Word having been unto God,
and God having been the Word
he having been, in the beginning unto God
all through his hand became:
and without him
not even one being whatever became.
In him life became
— the life having the light of the son of humanity.
And the light enlightened the darkness
and the darkness overtook it not.

• Note how the compound verbs authenticate the eternal existence of the Word.

2 Tima Theaus 4:3

For the time being they hear not healthy doctrine
— but as to their pantings they abound to soul doctors*
who excite their hearing.

*psychologists

1 Petros 3:19

. . . and preaching to the souls being held in sheol . . .

• Note how this translation gives meaning to the prophecies of David, as well as to the ministry of Yah Shua during his entombment.

• Premier Gold Hard Cover Edition with Summaries.

• ISBN 0—9631951—6—6: $29.95 •

**NEW! Version 3.0**

## exeGeses BIBLES CDRom

**Cuts your research to the bone.**
**Eliminates the fat,**
**Gets you to the meat of the Word.**

- **Imagine having every Literal Translation & Transliteration of Scripture at your computer tips:**
- **NEW 3.0 Version with complete search engine.**

- **The exeGeses *parallel BIBLE*,** with
- **The exeGeses *ready research BIBLE*,** and
- **The exeGeses *companion BIBLE*,** side by side:
- ***The ARAMAIC NEW COVENANT, PLUS***
- ***The ARAMAIC NEW COVENANT INTERLINEAR***

— the equivalent of a 5,500 page book.

• Now, for the first time, you have the Literal Translation & Transliteration on one line, followed by the Aramaic root, the part of speech, and its synonymns on the following lines.

- Windows, MAC
- ISBN 0—9631951—7—4: List: . . . . . . . . . . . $99.95 •
- With any exeGeses Bible: . . . . . . . . . . . . $29.95 *